Inclusion

The Practicing Administrator's Leadership Series
Jerry J. Herman and Janice L. Herman, Editors

ROADMAPS
TO SUCCESS

Other Titles in This Series Include:

The Path to School Leadership: A Portable Mentor
Lee G. Bolman and Terrence E. Deal

Holistic Quality: Managing, Restructuring, and Empowering Schools
Jerry J. Herman

Selecting, Managing, and Marketing Technologies
Jamieson A. McKenzie

Individuals With Disabilities: Implementing the Newest Laws
Patricia F. First and Joan L. Curcio

Violence in the Schools: How to Proactively Prevent and Defuse It
Joan L. Curcio and Patricia F. First

Women in Administration: Facilitators for Change
L. Nan Restine

Power Learning in the Classroom
Jamieson A. McKenzie

Computers: Literacy and Learning
A Primer for Administrators
George E. Marsh II

Restructuring Schools: Doing It Right
Mike M. Milstein

Reporting Child Abuse:
A Guide to Mandatory Requirements for School Personnel
Karen L. Michaelis

Handbook on Gangs in Schools:
Strategies to Reduce Gang-Related Activities
Shirley R. Lal, Dhyan Lal, and Charles M. Achilles

Conflict Resolution: Building Bridges
Neil H. Katz and John W. Lawyer

Resolving Conflict Successfully: Needed Knowledge and Skills
Neil H. Katz and John W. Lawyer

Preventing and Managing Conflict in Schools
Neil H. Katz and John W. Lawyer

Secrets of Highly Effective Meetings
Maria M. Shelton and Laurie K. Bauer

(see back cover for additional titles)

Inclusion
Are We Abandoning or Helping Students?

Sandra Alper, Patrick J. Schloss
Susan K. Etscheidt
and Christine A. Macfarlane

CORWIN PRESS, INC.
A Sage Publications Company
Thousand Oaks, California

For information address:

Corwin Press, Inc.
A Sage Publications Company
2455 Teller Road
Thousand Oaks, California 91320

SAGE Publications Ltd.
6 Bonhill Street
London EC2A 4PU
United Kingdom

SAGE Publications India Pvt. Ltd.
M-32 Market
Greater Kailash I
New Delhi 110 048 India

Printed in the United States of America

Library of Congress Cataloging-in-Publication Data

Inclusion: are we abandoning or helping students? / Sandra Alper . . . [et al.].
        p.   cm. — (Roadmaps to success)
    Includes bibliographical references (p. 67-77).
    ISBN 0-8039-6249-5 (pbk.)
        1. Handicapped children—Education—United States.
    2. Mainstreaming in education—United States.   I. Alper, Sandra K.
    II. Series.
LC4015.I48   1995
371.9'046—dc20   95-15806

This book is printed on acid-free paper.

95 96 97 98 99 10 9 8 7 6 5 4 3 2 1

Corwin Press Production Editor: S. Marlene Head

Contents

Foreword

Inclusion is one of the hottest and most controversial topics facing schools today. The authors of *Inclusion: Are We Abandoning or Helping Students?* have produced a short, easily read book that provides a comprehensive overview of inclusion.

Chapter 1 explores the history of inclusion and the legal context within which inclusion is taking place today. Various aspects of inclusion, such as a continuum of services, the least restrictive environment, full inclusion, and inclusion opportunities, are discussed. Chapter 2 presents insights into the roles and responsibilities of each member of an inclusion team.

Chapter 3 outlines appropriate inclusion practices for students with mild disabilities. Lesson objectives, skill and concept acquisition and practice, skill evaluation, approaches to classroom management, goal setting, progress monitoring, instructional methods, and other evaluative techniques are discussed. Chapter 4 addresses inclusion practices for students with severe disabilities. Information is included about students' characteristics, methods of assessment, curriculum modifications, instructional strategies, transitioning of students into inclusive settings, and technological aids.

Finally, for those readers who wish to delve more deeply into the issues surrounding inclusion, the authors provide numerous references as well as an annotated bibliography of primary resources.

For educators who have concerns about how to implement a program of student inclusion, this brief book should prove to be an invaluable resource. It provides a wide variety of practical advice for implementing—and maintaining—programs of inclusion in the schools of this country.

JERRY J. HERMAN
JANICE L. HERMAN
Series Co-Editors

About the Authors

Sandra Alper is Professor and Chair of the Department of Special Education at the University of Northern Iowa. She received a Ph.D. in special education from the University of Iowa. She has worked as a public school teacher of students with mental retardation and as coordinator of programs in severe disabilities in the Department of Special Education at the University of Missouri—Columbia. Dr. Alper has directed and codirected several federally funded model demonstration and personnel preparation grants in the areas of severe disabilities and dual diagnosis. She also served as codirector of a community-based supported living program for youth with mental retardation and challenging behaviors. Dr. Alper is a frequent contributor to the professional literature. The focus of her teaching, research, and consultation is on teaching functional skills that enable individuals with moderate to severe disabilities to fully participate in their schools and communities.

Patrick J. Schloss is Assistant Vice President for Graduate Studies and Research at Bloomsburg University. He obtained his doctorate from the University of Wisconsin and previously chaired the special education department at the University of Missouri. Dr. Schloss is a frequent contributor to the special education and rehabilitation psychology literature. He has published more than 150 articles addressing the educational development and social adjustment of students with disabilities. He has also authored several texts that are used in special education methods and issues courses. Dr. Schloss is also an active consultant to school and residential programs for persons with disabilities.

Susan K. Etscheidt is Associate Professor of Special Education at the University of Northern Iowa (UNI) and the Coordinator of Programs for Children with Behavioral Disorders K-6. She teaches courses in the area of behavioral disorders, behavior management, and mainstreaming. In addition to her involvement in the teacher training program at UNI, Dr. Etscheidt conducts numerous inservices and workshops for practitioners. Her research interests and activities include cognitive-behavioral management, social skill assessment and instruction, integration of children with learning and behavior problems, and special education law. Dr. Etscheidt has taught children with severe learning, behavior, and mental disabilities in a variety of settings. She is currently directing a peer-to-peer program to teach vocationally related social skills.

Christine A. Macfarlane is Assistant Professor and Coordinator of the Mental Disabilities program at the University of Northern Iowa. She came to UNI in 1991 from Utah State University, where she received both an M.S. (1982) and a Ph.D. (1990) in special education. While at USU, she held positions as a clinical demonstration teacher, clinical instructor, project codirector, and research assistant professor. Her extensive experience in working with students with severe disabilities as a classroom teacher provides a firm foundation for her work in preservice and inservice teacher training and research. Dr. Macfarlane's research interests include nonaversive behavioral management, functional communication, data-based decision making, and the use of technology for teachers and students with disabilities. She has coauthored three data-based expert systems and numerous research articles and book chapters on these subjects.

Introduction

Our children are the future. The way in which we educate our children will significantly shape the future. Few issues related to how we educate children have elicited as much controversy as the inclusion of students with disabilities in the full mainstream of general education. Inclusion is an important issue because it affects virtually all stakeholders in education, including children with and without disabilities and their families, special and general education teachers, administrators, related services personnel, school staff, and the general public.

In the text, we have tried to avoid the emotionality sometimes injected into arguments for or against inclusionary schooling. Our goal is to clearly define full inclusion, articulate the rationale for this practice, and present a variety of practical strategies for implementation. As authors, we attempted to avoid using a great deal of technical language. An annotated bibliography is included for readers who want to study inclusion further.

In Chapter 1, Patrick J. Schloss provides the historical and legal context in which the concept of inclusion evolved. Key terms are defined, and the benefits of inclusion for students with and without disabilities are explained.

Using examples taken from her own experiences in the public schools, Christine A. Macfarlane describes the roles and responsibilities of inclusion team members in Chapter 2. Collaboration between general and special educators is critical to the success of inclusion. Dr. Macfarlane explains how team members representing different disciplines can work together and share ownership of the educational program.

The final two chapters of this text focus on strategies that can be implemented in regular education settings in which students with and without disabilities are served. In Chapter 3, Susan K. Etscheidt addresses ways in which the needs of students with mild disabilities may be met in the regular classroom. Strategies that may be used to deal with inappropriate behaviors in the classroom are emphasized. In Chapter 4, Sandra Alper addresses students with severe disabilities in inclusive school settings. Both Chapters 3 and 4 emphasize practical strategies for student assessment, curriculum modification, and instruction.

The editors of this text were wise to have targeted school principals as the primary audience because they play such a critical leadership role in inclusion. We hope other practitioners will find the book to be useful as well.

The Context: How Far Have We Come and Where Are We Going?

Full Inclusion

Education and social services for persons with disabilities have evolved through an extensive and curious history. Survival was the dominant theme of ancient cultures. Individuals with disabilities were not able to gather food or protect themselves. If kept alive, this burden was extended to other family members, placing them "at risk" for harm or starvation. Consequently, eugenics through abandonment or more direct means was liberally practiced.

Superstition exerted a major influence on the treatment of persons with disabilities in the Middle Ages. Disabilities were explained as resulting from the sins of mothers and fathers. Abnormal behavior was attributed to demonic possession. Treatment often involved burning, whipping, stoning, and other harsh forms of punishment. Exorcism was also used to "purify the soul" and cast out demons responsible for norm-violating behavior.

More recent accounts emphasize the role of science in understanding and treating disabilities. Medical practitioners and researchers have considered the role of biological functions such as genetics, trauma, diet, and disease in the development of physical, cognitive, and emotional disorders. Behavioral researchers have focused on the effects of environment and learning on human adaptation. Sociologists have considered the influence of the broader society in accepting or rejecting deviance.

Although research remains a constant theme in current practices for persons with disabilities, increased attention has been placed on social policy. At no time in history has greater attention been paid to including persons with disabilities in all aspects of life.

As will be discussed later, social policy in the United States and other developed nations emphasizes the full integration of all persons regardless of skin color, sex, physical, or cognitive disability. Substantial attention has been paid to minimizing both physical and political barriers that exclude any individual from the mainstream of society.

In no way is this emphasis more strongly identified than in the movement toward full inclusion in America's schools. A major focus in today's schools is on making the opportunities available to general society accessible to all learners regardless of physical and cognitive limitations. Although the movement toward inclusion has evoked controversy among scholars, administrators, service providers, and family members, it has substantial political and legislative support.

This book is written to provide school administrators a concise resource for understanding and participating in inclusion. Highlighted are the benefits and liabilities of inclusion, professionals responsible for promoting inclusion and their associated roles, best practices for promoting inclusion among mildly disabled learners, and best practices for severely disabled students. We will begin by defining essential terms used in policy debate and professional practice.

Critical Terms

Continuum of Services

Students with disabilities often require a variety of support services. These may be minimally intrusive such as corrective lenses, tutorial assistance, and special scheduling. They may also be highly intrusive such as special instructional placement, use of extraordinary-care aides, and participation in a substantially altered curriculum. The continuum of services is an array of supports ranging from least to most restrictive.

The continuum of services includes all school features relevant to a student's educational progress. One of the most basic and important features is the educational placement. The least to most restrictive continuum generally includes regular class, regular class with consultative assistance, regular class with part-time resource room assistance, part day in special classes, full day in special classes, special school, and hospital or homebound placement.

Least Restrictive Environment

Federal law and numerous court cases emphasize that students be placed in the least restrictive environment appropriate to their educational characteristics. With respect to educational placement, students who can be educated in less restrictive regular class placements should not be placed in segregated classes. Students unable to benefit from regular class placement, but able to gain from participation in special classes, should not be placed in segregated special schools.

Federal mandate defines least restrictive environment as the assurance by public schools that removal of a student with disabilities from regular classes occurs only when the nature or severity of the disability is such that education in the regular education setting with the use of special aids and support services does not achieve satisfactory results (Education for All Handicapped Children Act, 1976).

The principle of least restrictive environment emphasizes that initial placement consideration is the regular classroom, and subsequent placements are made only when the regular class placement is deemed to be ineffective. Further, a continuum of services must be available when making an educational placement. A thorough diagnostic evaluation must be conducted to establish an appropriate match between the learner's characteristics and placement. Finally, it requires frequent review so that movement can be made to less restrictive settings as the student's social and academic skills develop.

Inclusion

Inclusion is the practice of providing educational experiences for persons with disabilities in the same school and classroom that they would attend were they not disabled. In most cases, this would be regular classes in their neighborhood school—the same school that their siblings attended or will attend, and the same classes that their neighbors of the same age attend.

The principle of inclusion is based on several tenets. First, students are more similar than dissimilar and all can learn regardless of disability. Second, learning often occurs through participating with and modeling competent peers. Third, diverse instructional supports that allow a student to overcome disabilities that detract from learning can be provided in the regular classroom. Fourth, everyone benefits from including students with diverse learning and behavioral features in the same classroom.

Advocates of inclusion suggest that in rare cases, students may require supports that cannot be implemented in regular class settings. However, the continuum of services is still made available through adherence to the principle of least restrictive environment.

Full Inclusion

Full inclusion involves adherence to the principle of inclusion without exception. Proponents of full inclusion recommend eliminating the continuum of services and argue that the tenets underlying inclusion apply to all learners without exception. In other words, full inclusion would make all special class placements unnecessary, as all learners would be served in neighborhood schools with their same-aged peers. Special education services would address supports needed to promote learning in the regular class and school.

Full inclusion is inconsistent with consideration of the least restrictive environment appropriate to a learner's characteristics. If all students are fully included in the same classes as their neighbors and peers, there is no need for more restrictive segregated classes or schools. Consequently, the continuum of services would cease to exist in schools that fully included all learners.

At the present time, federal law mandates the provision of a continuum of services. It further requires the careful study of students for placement in the least restrictive environment appropriate to their educational characteristics. Finally, it requires periodic review to assure the appropriateness of a given placement as the individual's learning and behavioral features develop. Policies and procedures recommended in this text are consistent with these mandates.

Although we recognize that full inclusion may be interpreted as inconsistent with the law, we believe that improved inclusion practices will reduce placements outside of the neighborhood school to the point that schools will approach the standard of full inclusion for the vast majority of students.

Inclusion Opportunities

A number of opportunities for inclusion exist throughout the school day. The most structured of these is *participation in required courses* meeting the same expectations as others in class. This may occur with or without extraordinary support. Typical support may include the use of a paraprofessional, structured peer tutoring activity, or the use of special technology.

A similarly structured inclusion opportunity involves *participation in nonrequired courses with modified expectations*. Again, extraordinary support may be arranged by the teacher or a consultant. The major difference from the preceding inclusion opportunity is that although the student is educated in the same setting and at the same time as other learners, he or she may focus on different objectives. Curriculum differences may range from focusing on totally different objectives (e.g., the regular class works on division while the student with disabilities focuses on subtraction) to objectives that differ slightly in depth or breadth (e.g., the regular class works on division including practical exercises while the student with disabilities focuses solely on the division algorithm).

A less structured opportunity involves *inclusion in extracurricular activities*. These may include participating in interscholastic sports, student government, library club, school newspaper, Scouting, and so on. As with the other forms of inclusion, participation in extracurricular activities can be supported by paraprofessionals, special peer arrangements, and the use of technology. In can also occur without extraordinary support.

The least structured inclusion activities involve basic *social participation*. In general, there are no specific goals or objectives. No special arrangements are made to enhance the potential for acquiring specific skills. Examples of social inclusion include hallway passage, lunchroom use, playground or recreational participation, and membership in extracurricular organizations or sports. Again, these activities can occur with or without extraordinary support.

Legal Foundations for Inclusion

Several federal laws dictate the manner in which learners with disabilities are identified, assessed, placed, and taught. These laws include the Rehabilitation Act of 1973, the Education for All Handicapped Children Act of 1975, the Education of the Handicapped Act of 1986, and the Individuals With Disabilities Education Act of 1990. The major implications of these laws for inclusion practices are as follows:

1. Special education services suitable to the needs of the disabled student must be provided at no cost to the student or family.

2. Parents must receive written notification prior to the school's conducting a case study evaluation that may determine eligibility for special education services.

3. Individualized, comprehensive, and nondiscriminatory assessment must be provided for the purpose of identifying the learner's unique characteristics and needs.

4. An individualized education program (IEP) must be developed annually for students with disabilities. The IEP must contain a statement of current performance levels, annual goals and short-term objectives, specific services to be provided, extent of participation in regular education settings, projected date for initiation of services, expected duration of services, objective criteria, and evaluation procedures.

5. An individualized family service plan (IFSP) must be provided to children with disabilities who are 3 to 5 years of age. The IFSP must contain the child's current performance levels, family strengths and weaknesses, anticipated outcomes, necessary services, timelines for initiating and completing services, the name of

the service manager, and methods for transitioning the child to appropriate services.

6. An individual transition plan (ITP) must be included with the IEPs of adolescents and young adults. The ITP is developed with the assistance of community-based vocational rehabilitation personnel. It complements the IEP by adding skills and services needed to support the transition from school to work.

7. Beyond specific educational services, students with disabilities are entitled to receive necessary related services. These include developmental, corrective, and other support services needed for the child or youth to benefit fully from the educational program. They may include transportation; counseling; medical evaluation; and physical, occupational, and recreation therapy.

8. Educational services must be provided in the least restrictive setting appropriate to the student's educational characteristics.

9. Finally, parents and guardians are entitled to due process when disputes regarding the appropriateness of the educational program occur.

These provisions highlight the manner in which special education services are to be provided. Emphasis is placed on the identification of students with disabilities, careful appraisal of the student, the development of an individualized plan for addressing the student needs, and parental participation in developing and carrying out the plan. An overriding focus of these services is that they be provided in the least restrictive setting appropriate to the learner's educational characteristics.

The Individuals With Disabilities Act (1990) specifically states that

> To the extent appropriate, handicapped children, including children in public or private institutions or other care facilities, are educated with children who are not handicapped, and that special classes, separate schooling, or other removal of handicapped children from the regular education environments occurs only when the nature or severity of the handicap is such that education in regular classes with the use of supplementary aids and services cannot be achieved satisfactorily.

Identifying the Least Restrictive
and Most Inclusive Placement

As emphasized above, federal law clearly mandates that educational services occur in the least restrictive setting appropriate to the child's educational characteristics. There has been substantial debate, however, on how the least restrictive environment should be defined for individual learners. As noted earlier, advocates such as Stainback, Stainback, and Forest (1989) take an extreme position by identifying the regular class setting with nondisabled peers as the only appropriate environment for special education services. We believe, however, that a more moderate position is warranted.

Maloney (1994) has reviewed every inclusion-related decision rendered by federal courts since 1989. Her review clarifies schools' responsibilities for serving students with disabilities.

The following procedures have been held by the courts to violate the least restrictive provision of federal law:

1. Endorsing a blanket policy or practice regarding the segregation of individual or groups of students with disabilities
2. Avoiding the use of supplementary aids and services for promoting regular classroom placement (e.g., consultative support, resource room support, use of extraordinary-care aides, use of behavioral programming, and development of unique instructional arrangements)
3. Using cost of regular education placement, without foundation, as a criterion for adopting a segregated placement
4. Excluding disruptive children from mainstream settings without demonstrating the ineffectiveness of behavior modification strategies

Conversely, the following conditions have been held by the courts to mitigate against including a child in a regular class placement:

1. No amount of support allows the child to make acceptable educational or social progress in the regular classroom.
2. Despite the use of supplementary aids and services, the general learning environment is adversely affected to the extent that other children are deprived of effective instruction.

3. The cost of serving a child with disabilities in a regular classroom will substantially and adversely affect resources available to others in the district.

4. Curriculum modification required for the child with disabilities will produce two separate classes in the same room and/or result in the child's being instructionally segregated from others in the class.

Maloney (1994) notes that beyond these legal findings, the Office of Special Education and Rehabilitative Services (OSERS) supports the notion of serving individuals with disabilities alongside their nondisabled peers. As we stated earlier, however, OSERS emphasizes the importance of complying with the least restrictive environment provision of federal law. Placements must be determined only after the careful study of each individual child or youth. Some students with disabilities may require placements outside of the regular class. Therefore, the continuum of services must be maintained.

Positive Presumption Standard

One of the stronger standards for affording human rights in America is the standard of *positive presumption*. This standard emphasizes that we are afforded human rights as a basic condition of birth. Denial of these rights occurs only when it is determined that the loss of liberty is in the best interests of the individual or society.

Unfortunately, the presence of a disability often alters social judgment and improperly shifts the standard from positive to *negative presumption*. Negative presumption involves the restriction of rights until an individual demonstrates the ability to benefit from liberties assumed to be guaranteed nondisabled individuals. As emphasized previously, due process rights under federal law require that standards of positive presumption apply to learners with disabilities. That is, regardless of the severity of handicapping conditions, an individual is entitled to free access to all educational programs serving nondisabled individuals until it is demonstrated that the access is not in the best interest of the learner or others. Even then, a forum is provided under law for the formal adjudication of differences between the school's willingness to provide services and the student's and family members' interest in receiving the services.

Value of Inclusive Educational Practices

Aside from legal reasons, a number of strong reasons exist for including students with disabilities in general educational programs. Although many of these address the needs of the individual with disabilities, a number also relate to the interests of students who are not disabled. We will address both values in this section.

Students Who Are Not Disabled

In the past, students in general education programs have had little opportunity to interact with students with disabilities. As a consequence, they have had few opportunities to learn from such individuals. Inclusion offers the nondisabled student an opportunity to develop an appreciation for the complexity of human characteristics. Students who have not had these experiences may be surprised to learn that speech problems that accompany cerebral palsy do not necessarily indicate limited intelligence, cognitive impairment need not affect social development, and sensory impairment need not interfere with skill in motor activity.

Students with disabilities may teach nondisabled learners to go beyond dysfunctional stereotypes. All students with behavior disorders are not aggressive. Students with learning disabilities can be highly capable in some academic areas. Students with mental retardation may be outstanding citizens and neighbors.

Inclusion may also result in nondisabled students developing an appreciation for individual differences. Nondisabled students may learn that diversity in an inclusive classroom adds richness to the educational experience. They learn that all individuals have strengths and weaknesses, though no two individuals are the same. Some will excel in certain academic areas whereas some will excel in others. Some will be capable in certain sports whereas some will perform well in others. Some will be highly social whereas some will be more withdrawn.

Inclusion may teach nondisabled students about handicapping conditions. Exposure to a youngster who is blind may cause other students to gain accurate information about blindness. For example, they may learn that many individuals who are considered to be blind have some residual sight. They may learn that the debilitating effects of blindness can be minimized through the use of modern technology. Finally, they may recognize that visual impairment need not affect intelligence, social functioning, or other characteristics. Most important, students who are not disabled may learn that regardless of the complexity or severity of a handicapping condition, all human beings have more characteristics in common than they have differences. Regardless of disability, a majority of students wish to be accepted by others. A majority wish to achieve and have successes recognized by others. Students may learn that the presence of a disability does not eliminate basic emotional needs.

Students Who Are Disabled

There is little question about the power of observational learning. Much of what we learn is gained by observing others. Children and youths who grow up in an environment supported by competent peers and adults are likely to develop similar characteristics. Conversely, individuals who grow up in a setting with inappropriate models may acquire the inappropriate responses of these models. Therefore, a major advantage of inclusion is that it provides opportunities for students with disabilities to learn through interactions with nondisabled individuals.

Similarly, students with disabilities may be motivated to explore school and community activities (e.g., sports, school organizations, Scouting, park district events, etc.) because their friends are involved. Beyond simply becoming aware of an activity and choosing to go, the individual may also benefit from the guidance of nondisabled peers during the activity. This may have the related effect of helping students with disabilities to make a successful transition to adult life. Career awareness, use of community transportation, awareness of community resources, and so on, may all be effective by-products of participating with nondisabled peers in after-school events.

Students participating in integrated settings are likely to benefit from the stronger social norms established by their peers. Peer pressure and peer modeling may cause the child or youth with disabilities to conform to a social code established by the general classroom. Attire, language, interpersonal interactions, and so on may all be favorably influenced by this informal and subtle peer group behavior.

Finally, though precise figures are not available, inclusion programs are likely to be less expensive than programs that segregate students with disabilities. As an example, the cost of self-contained special education services in New York City currently exceeds $20,000 a year per pupil. It is highly likely that inclusive programs can be constructed for a majority of students with a budget well below this figure.

Conclusions

We have attempted to place the ideas contained in this guide into a historical and social context. We have emphasized that special services have evolved from orientations of survival, to superstition, to science, and now to service. The major focus on the current service movement is on the integration of persons with disabilities into the general pattern of daily life expected for all citizens. This emphasis has spawned the inclusion movement. Within this movement, we expect that to the extent possible, learners with disabilities should be served in the same setting as their nondisabled peers.

We emphasized that there is a strong legislative and litigative base for inclusion. The Education for All Handicapped Children Act (1976) and subsequent amendments highlight the importance of educating learners with special needs in the least restrictive environment appropriate to their educational characteristics. In most cases, this will be the regular education classroom. In other cases, it may be part-time special class placement. In others, it may be segregated classrooms. The decision regarding the appropriateness of a placement is based on the careful study of the individual student. In any case, we advocated the use of a positive presumption that the learner can benefit from regular class placement, with subsequent data being used to support alternatives.

Finally, we emphasized that both the student with disabilities and students with typical characteristics benefit from inclusion. In general, students with disabilities benefit from having normal individuals as social and academic models. They are likely to experience a wider range of community opportunities as a result of interacting with normal peers. Finally, they are likely to benefit from the enhanced motivation that results from aspiring to be like their peers.

Students who are not disabled are likely to become more aware and understanding of individuals with diverse learning and behavioral features. They may learn that human beings are complex and that the presence of a disability in one area can not be generalized to all aspects of an individual's functioning.

It is important to note that inclusion is not simply placing a student with disabilities in his or her neighborhood school without providing supports needed to ensure success. The major element of success is the quality of personnel who are available to contribute to the student's development. In the next chapter we will consider the service providers that may be involved in inclusive education.

Roles and Responsibilities
of Inclusive Teams

The educational team sat around a work table in the classroom. Their task: to generate an appropriate individualized educational program (IEP) for Jamie, a child with severe disabilities. All team members, except one, concentrated on the task at hand. The parent voiced concerns, provided relevant information, and assisted in determining priorities for the coming year. The teacher strove to translate those priorities into functional goals and objectives that would guide Jamie's education for the coming year. Related service staff contributed their expertise. The speech-language pathologist suggested augmentative communication strategies that could continue and identified several options that merited evaluation. The occupational therapist (OT) noted potential options for alternate positioning to enhance the acquisition of skills and give Jamie needed changes throughout the instructional day. The physical therapist (PT) reported progress in learning to stand and walk. He felt strongly that therapy should take place in the classroom. Each professional suggested possible adaptations to increase Jamie's independence and encouraged Mom to try certain strategies at home. Mom volunteered to make age-appropriate cover-ups (bibs) for

Jamie to wear while eating lunch in the cafeteria. All were committed to helping Jamie become as independent as possible and included in school activities. The lone observer was the building principal, Mr. Jones. He sat at the end of the table, slightly apart from the group, stacking blocks.

Unfortunately, this is a true story. Mr. Jones had little experience with students with severe disabilities. His presence as the local education agency (LEA) representative was required at such meetings, but he had nothing to contribute other than his signature. Mr. Jones was not a bad person. In fact, he had a reputation within the school district as a good administrator in a "tough" school. However, his latest assignment had found him ill prepared. At this point, late in his career, he was not even sure that children "like this" belonged in a regular school. On the one hand, his behavior was somewhat appropriate. Mr. Jones had no insight into Jamie's education, so he simply stayed out of the way. On the other hand, his active support would have facilitated a truly dynamic school climate that moved beyond tolerance to true acceptance and reached forward toward a future where children of all abilities could live, learn, and play together.

Inclusion, a grassroots movement driven by parental dissatisfaction with the current delivery system and the conviction that all children should be educated together, has captured the attention of educators and the general public alike. The ensuing controversy has sparked debate and discussion in a variety of places, from small-town cafés, advocacy organizations, professional conferences, school board meetings, and faculty meetings to university campuses and the courts. As I observe and participate in the discussion, conduct research, and train teachers, I am struck by the uncanny resemblance to the educational delivery system of rural Nebraska that I knew 30 years ago. Many eighth-grade students graduated from one- or two-room country schools where one or two teachers taught all children. Two major differences exist. First, students with severe disabilities then did not attend school, whereas today, all children, regardless of disability, are entitled to a free and appropriate education. Second, back then there was just *one* teacher; now there is a team.

The Inclusion Team

Teaching students with disabilities in inclusive settings is a multifaceted task that cannot be accomplished by just one person. Inclusive education happens when a team of mutually supportive players pledges to provide best practices for a student with disabilities. Depending on the disability and level of student need, a team with unique but complementary skills will be brought on board to guide, advocate for, and implement this student's educational program. More than any other element, the need for team effort to manage, deliver, and support a student's inclusive education is a drastic change for regular educators.

Traditionally, regular educators have operated in a fairly autonomous environment. One teacher assumed responsibility for a classroom with 25 students. Interactions with administrators, other teachers, and consultants generally took place outside the classroom. Administrators were often viewed as authority figures rather than collaborators. Although teachers frequently planned activities or scheduled student exchanges together, they infrequently found themselves working side by side in the classroom as a team. Consultation and inservice training occurred during times when students were not present. When a student required additional services, such as speech therapy, the professional, in keeping with a clinical model, removed the student from the classroom.

The traditional model is driven by circumstances and needs rather than unwillingness. Teachers cannot leave the classroom; students require constant supervision. Dipping into an available pool of substitutes is neither practical nor feasible. Furthermore, it is difficult to conduct articulation therapy in a classroom with 24 other students.

Special education, however, has always followed a team format. For one reason, federal legislation mandated it. Furthermore, students with multiple disabilities required a number of related services. A student's program did not come together unless there was joint effort and cooperation from all members of the team. How that team functioned—the guiding paradigm—has changed over time.

The Multidisciplinary Approach

Initially, teams followed a *multidisciplinary* approach (see Figure 2.1). Using a medical or clinical model to guide the service delivery, each team member individually evaluated a student, designed a prescriptive program, and implemented that program. Team members knew that other professionals were involved in the student's education but rarely interacted with each other and seldom shared information. Most, with prompting from the special education teacher, kept the teacher and parents apprised of what was going on. The annual IEP meeting was used as a vehicle to report results and present next year's schedule for therapy (e.g., three times per week for 15 minutes) along with objectives to address generic skill deficits (e.g., improve walking).

The Interdisciplinary Approach

As the delivery of services to students with disabilities began to shift from a pullout medical or clinical model, the team paradigm shifted to an *interdisciplinary* approach (see Figure 2.1). Instead of teaching skills in isolation, therapy was geared toward functional skills (e.g., climbing the stairs in the hallway or on the slide) and was less fragmented. Interactions with fellow team members became more collegial. Each team member shared information and suggested strategies for incorporating important goals and objectives across disciplines. The speech-language pathologist might report that the student needed practice answering "what" questions while the physical therapist demonstrated the correct method for assisting the student to walk with support. Now or then, the speech-language pathologist might walk the student to a therapy session with the right kind of support. During therapy, the physical therapist might engage the student in conversation by asking such questions as "What's your favorite TV show?" Even though therapy might take place in the classroom within the context of functional skill acquisition, team members still delivered services to the student individually.

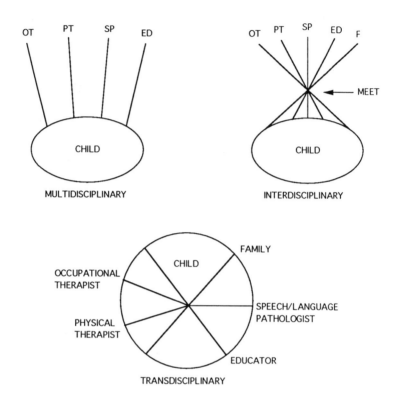

Figure 2.1. A Visual Representation of the Three Team Paradigms: Multidisciplinary, Interdisciplinary, and Transdisciplinary

The Transdisciplinary Approach

With the shift from a medical model to integrated therapy, providing services to students with disabilities required a consolidated effort. With the *transdisciplinary* approach (see Figure 2.1), the entire team focuses its efforts on the student and his or her family. Team members continue to share discipline-specific information and target functional skills. However, they now emphasize blending therapy needs into a consolidated program based on natural routines that exist within the students' environments. A walking program turns into a mobility program when the student gets off the bus and needs to get to the classroom. The opportunity to greet others along the way incorporates a communication goal.

Roles and Responsibilities of Team Members

The transdisciplinary model is the paradigm of choice to guide the inclusive team process. Throughout the process, team members assume flexible roles called *role transition* (Garland, McGonigel, Frank, & Buck, 1989). Team members who develop additional expertise in their discipline extend their role. *Role extension* may be accomplished by attending professional conferences, participating in staff development, and reading journals and other professional literature. When team members learn basic terminology and practices associated with another member's discipline, their own role is enriched. Through *role enrichment*, a physical therapist might demonstrate to other team members the correct terms to describe different body positions (e.g., prone: on the stomach). *Role expansion* occurs when one team member becomes proficient enough in another discipline to offer knowledgeable suggestions. Special education teachers frequently become quite expert in the correct positioning of their students. Occasionally, a team member will trade places with another team member and, with supervision, provide relevant information. A parent who demonstrates positioning during a play activity to the occupational therapist is engaging in *role exchange*. Sometimes, one team member must support another team member, who will then transmit his or her discipline-specific knowledge and information. A teacher who shares dietary information with the parents is an example of *role release*. The final transition occurs during *role support*. This is characterized by informal encouragement and additional consultation to maintain discipline-specific skills among team members.

Who ends up on an inclusive team for a specific student depends totally on the needs of the student and the people who have the expertise to meet those needs. Initially, some team members will volunteer and be openly excited about working with a student in an inclusive setting. Others will be drafted reluctantly. Teachers and other professionals who are open to change, constantly striving to improve themselves and willing to try innovative solutions, frequently self-select into working with students who present a challenge. Otherwise, capable people can be approached and encouraged to accept such a challenge. Only under the most unusual circumstances should a teacher be forced to accept a student with disabilities into a regular class.

Strong administrative support fosters success in an inclusive setting. However, administrators, teachers, professionals, and other team members do best when they "buy in" to the concept of inclusion rather than "obey" edicts. To facilitate open communication, teachers need time and opportunities to talk with other teachers who have participated in this process and made it work. Candid, straightforward information about the struggles and the joys of inclusive education must be shared. As a responsible administrator and team member, a proactive approach is always preferred to a reactive approach.

In addition to a proactive approach, planning is essential to successful inclusive education. Planning must occur frequently on a formal (e.g., meetings) or informal (e.g., classroom) basis. Finding time for planning is one of the biggest deterrents to providing a consistent program. When teachers use their planning time exclusively for one student, they lose out on critical planning time for the rest of their students. Traditional school schedules do not allow enough time during the day for teachers, professionals, and other key players to exchange information, observe one another, and make decisions about future strategies and interventions, even though this is one of the most important variables affecting the outcome. Flexible, creative options must be found to solve this problem.

By nature of the word inclusion, inclusive education happens within the context of an environment rich in people. These people provide meaningful opportunities for friendship, support, and socialization. In addition to meeting a student's social needs, we must accommodate a student's desire to function independently in as many settings as possible. Independence translates into competence in motor, communication, social, academic, and life skills. Depending on the focus of a student's IEP and his or her personal needs, the transdisciplinary team could consist of the parents and student, school administrators, regular education teacher(s), special education teacher(s), consultant(s), paraprofessionals, occupational therapist, physical therapist, speech-language pathologist, school nurse, and same-age nondisabled peers. Other personnel, although not on the formal team, would have contact with the student (e.g., bus driver, cafeteria workers). The potential members of a team are depicted in Figure 2.2.

Although necessary, a team this large can intimidate parents. Too many professionals around a table or in a room can create a closed atmosphere in which they come across as "in charge," superior, and "knowing it all." Parents may end up feeling that they are treated as inferior, or just like their child; that is, they may feel that they "need fixing." Particularly in the beginning, teams may need to break up and meet with parents in smaller, less threatening, more cordial groups (Giangreco, Cloninger, & Iverson, 1993). As needed, important information can be transmitted to and from those meetings by the team leader. In fact, formal communication strategies among team members will enhance and facilitate the entire process.

The role of team leader can be assumed by one of several people. In some instances, this role can be played very well by a knowledgeable administrator or consultant. Most teams, however, rely on the special education teacher to serve as team leader. The team leader must organize meetings, maintain communication with the family and all members of the team, and facilitate exchanges of information. However, each team member must make a commitment to participate fully in the process. When communication occurs frequently, relevant information can pass back and forth between team members. Otherwise, someone may feel "out of the loop." Documents that can be routed, written communication (electronic or printed), telephone calls, and personal contacts are all appropriate communication strategies to keep team members informed and involved.

Whether the entire team meets or members of the team meet, the purpose will be either consultation or collaboration. As stated earlier, the role that a team member plays will change depending on the circumstances. When engaged in consultation, one team member will provide another team member with assistance that may be very technical or somewhat informal. For example, the school

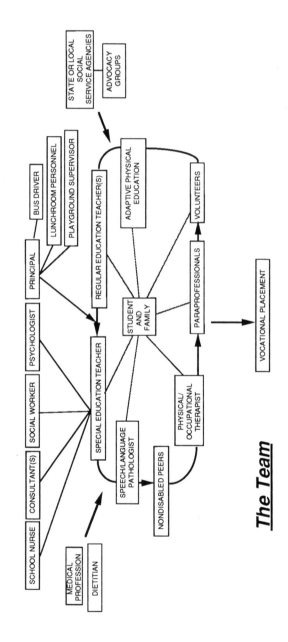

The Team

Figure 2.2. A Model of Potential Team Members for a Student in an Inclusive Educational Setting

nurse may need to train a paraprofessional to perform a clean intermittent catheterization procedure, or she may simply need to relay information about potential side effects of a current medication. Collaboration involves working together toward a common goal and, again, it may be quite informal or highly formalized. As an example, the fourth-grade teacher may have several students who are doing poorly in reading. Because the special education teacher must be in the classroom working on reading with the included student anyway, the teacher agrees to expand the reading group of one to include the other learners. The fourth-grade teacher benefits from the assistance as well as the opportunity to observe vicariously what the special education teacher does. Furthermore, the included student reaps the benefit of being in a group and the students who were having trouble are not pulled out of their classroom.

Because parents usually are the ones to insist on inclusion, establish the momentum, and drive the process, their role on the team is critical and can never be ignored or downplayed. The student's participation on the team is also vital. One of the basic philosophical tenets of inclusion is the student's right to personal choice. What better place to exercise personal choice than in the decision-making process. The belief that children should have friends and not be excluded from the normal social supports found in neighborhood schools is also a key philosophical tenet of inclusion. Adult team members should encourage the student's friends to offer support and ideas. Nondisabled peers can be an incredible source of positive thought and energy. Plus, early exposure to advocacy will most certainly affect their future interactions with persons with disabilities and their community.

The special education teacher, besides functioning as team leader, has many responsibilities when a student receives services in an inclusive setting. The special education teacher is most often the primary contact between parents and the school. Creating the student's schedule and ensuring that everyone follows it is a major job. Frequent changes, the bane of all classroom teachers, occur constantly. When changes happen (e.g., a school assembly), all affected persons must be notified and adjustments noted. Many times, this creates a domino effect. One schedule change creates the need for another, and so on. Along with providing individualized or small group instruction, special education teachers will need to teach others how to use the specialized materials and techniques that increase the likelihood that the included student will learn targeted skills. Finally, the special education teacher will be responsible for the data collection and documentation mandated by the IEP and necessary for future decision making.

The regular education teacher who provides the inclusive setting is another important member of the team. At the elementary level, this will generally be just one teacher with assistance from specialists (e.g., a music teacher). At the secondary level, the prevailing pattern will require the involvement of several teachers. Characteristics frequently found in these teachers are openness, creativity, innovation, and flexibility. For the most part, their role is to continue doing what they have always done, and usually very well. Their major responsibility is to recognize and accommodate the individual abilities of children in the classroom. Regular educators must also adapt to an increase in the number of people who will be in and out of their classrooms.

Because a student in an inclusive setting often needs added supports, many school districts hire a paraprofessional on a full- or part-time basis. Usually, the paraprofessional is supervised by the special education teacher. However, if the paraprofessional is hired in a specialty area (e.g., health aide), then the appropriate related service professional provides supervision. A paraprofessional can (a) work with the student on an individual basis, (b) collect data, (c) facilitate inclusion in a group, (d) supervise play or other social activities, (e) serve as a pipeline from the field to the team, and (f) assist with personal care. Many times, the paraprofessional establishes an extremely close relationship with the student and becomes a strong advocate. Unfortunately, this can sometimes lead to inappropriate ownership of the student's education. Although a paraprofessional must be able to work independently and is a valuable asset to the team, problems can arise if the paraprofessional moves beyond his or her role.

Students with disabilities usually need the extra services of more than one professional. Within their area of expertise, related service personnel will evaluate and prescribe a program for a student. In an inclusive setting, it is crucial that each professional work with other team members to infuse communication skills, social skills, and motor skills within natural routines and functional contexts. A student will learn to zip a coat much more easily when putting on a coat is followed by going out to recess. Likewise, communication or social skills that are needed across a multitude of settings will generalize more easily if taught within those contexts. Working with related service personnel is a two-way street. Teachers need access to the specific knowledge that specialists have, and because teaching is not their forte, related service personnel must collaborate with teachers to learn appropriate educational techniques.

The principal is the LEA representative and, therefore, the official keeper of the rules and regulations. Hopefully, unlike our "block stacker," the building principal is also the glue that holds the team together. The principal is sometimes a cheerleader and sometimes a public relations expert. Dealing with parents, children, teachers, staff, and the public comes with the territory. Sensitive, or perhaps more appropriate, sensible leadership should characterize this role. A fine balance must be maintained between what is right and good for students with disabilities and what is right and good for nondisabled peers or typical children. Responsibility for all never ceases.

Who, specifically, are members of the team is probably not as important as the fact that there is a team. Napoleon was quoted as saying, "There is somebody wiser than any of us, . . . and that is all of us." For inclusive teams, these words ring true.

3

Individuals With Mild Disabilities: Implementing Sound Practices

Cross-Disciplinary Contributions

The inclusion of students with mild disabilities into regular education classrooms will require effective cross-disciplinary collaboration. Collaboration is an ongoing style of interaction in which people voluntarily engage in shared program planning, implementation, evaluation, and overall program accountability (Bauwens & Hourcade, 1995). Teachers, parents, administrators, related service personnel, and students will need to accept the shared responsibility of educating students with mild disabilities in regular classrooms. Cross-disciplinary collaboration enables individuals with diverse expertise to share values, beliefs, information, educational tools, and professional skills. As school personnel collaborate, they pool their content knowledge and instructional skills to make available a more diverse set of instructional methodologies and a broader array of curricula for students with mild disabilities (Thousand, Villa, Paolucci-Whitcomb, & Nevin, 1992).

To successfully implement collaborative programs, traditional roles and responsibilities must be altered. *Regular educators* must modify teaching techniques, course content, evaluation, and grading procedures to accommodate the student's special learning needs. They must also carefully design classroom management procedures to encourage desirable, appropriate personal and interpersonal behavior while minimizing inappropriate, interfering behaviors from students with special needs. *Special educators* must expand their roles to include consultation and collaboration with regular educators on strategies to use with students with special needs within the context of the regular education classroom (Gersten, Darch, Davis, & George, 1991). This role may also involve cooperative teaching, whereby regular educators and supportive service personnel work jointly to develop and teach the instructional program in the mainstreamed setting (Bauwens, Hourcade, & Friend, 1989). *Related service personnel and therapists* must work in classrooms with teachers to provide direct and functional support services. *Parents* must realize that they are recognized as expert members of their children's educational teams. Parental awareness of their child's educational program and the level of coordination between home and school can make an important difference for many students in the mainstream (Lewis & Doorlag, 1987). *Students with disabilities* must assume some responsibility for their own educational outcomes. Students can provide the team with information about strengths and weaknesses, successful teaching strategies and materials, interests, hobbies and talents, and career goals (Van Reusen, Deshler, & Schumaker, 1989). Most important, *building administrators* must provide the necessary support for collaborative structures.

There are four types of administrative support required for effective cross-disciplinary collaboration:

1. *Vision and Agenda.* One of the most important types of support that the administrator can offer is providing a clear vision of how the school will educate all of its students and articulating the plans and actions to achieve those goals. The administrator must have an understanding of the role of each professional and stakeholder in providing equal educational opportunity to all students (Bauwens & Hourcade, 1995).

2. *Structure and Organization.* The administrator can facilitate cross-disciplinary collaboration by removing the barriers to change (i.e., administrative systems, workloads, time) and by providing a forum to explore, develop, and implement collaborative programs. This restructuring may include release and planning time for collaborators, scheduling changes, and various forms of technical assistance (e.g., decreasing class size, providing paraprofessional assistance) (Wood, 1992).

3. *Staff Training.* Although staff training is the key to instituting a collaborative approach, continuing education and ongoing professional development opportunities will also be necessary. Inservice training should address teacher-identified needs; employ competent personnel to deliver the training; be coordinated by the school districts, state DOE, teacher-training institutions, and professional organizations; offer incentives to educators to participate; use a variety of methods; and be evaluated. The administrator must also build time into teachers' schedules to allow collaborative problem solving, team meeting, peer coaching sessions, documentation of student progress and development, and adaptation of materials (Idol & West, 1987).

4. *Allocation of Resources.* The strongest expression of administrative support is the allocation of valued resources. A creative distribution and pooling of resources is essential to the implementation and maintenance of cross-disciplinary collaboration.

The cross-disciplinary team works cooperatively to provide services to students and their families. The purpose of collaboration is to expand the range of services available to students and their teachers, share the responsibility for educating all students, and coordinate the services provided. The specific services provided will vary depending on the needs of students and their families.

Some of the issues in collaboration include finding an approach that fits the climate of a particular school, gaining teacher support, arranging for release time, scheduling meetings, delegating decision-making responsibilities, providing teachers the recognition they deserve for team participation, and sustaining the momentum for collaborative programs (Gable, Korinek, & Laycock, 1993). As Gable et al. explain,

> In an era of diminishing resources and escalating demands, redefining the roles and responsibilities of school personnel poses a real challenge. The demands associated with peer collaboration provide both administrators and classroom teachers with legitimate grounds to resist. With the growing pressure to resolve the ills that many believe have befallen public education, the tremendous benefits of collaboration to general and special educators and administrators are not always easy to see. (p. 451)

Despite the myriad issues and barriers, collaboration provides an opportunity to increase the organizational and educational options available to students with disabilities. The collaborators become a school-based, child-oriented, problem-solving team. The inclusion of students with mild disabilities begins with the collaborative, problem-solving team asking a series of questions concerning assessment, methodology, behavior management, and evaluation:

1. How should we assess the student's needs?
2. Should we modify the curriculum?
3. How should we approach classroom management?
4. How should we evaluate our efforts?

How Should We Assess the Student's Needs?

As student variability is addressed in general education classrooms through collaborative arrangements, functional information about the student, his or her skills, and the effect of instruction on those skills is required (Howell, Fox, & Morehead, 1993). The best way to provide this functional information is to use curriculum-based measures (Shinn & Hubbard, 1992). Curriculum-based measures (CBM) provide local norms for judging the student's achievement status and instructional needs in various content areas. CBM evaluation also has "curriculum relevance" (i.e., the measures are drawn from the classroom curriculum; the results pinpoint specific skill deficits in that curriculum; the classroom teacher uses the information for instructional planning) (Howell et al., 1993). CBM methods are practical, educationally relevant, and of high utility to the collaborative team. The results confirm the student's instructional level and response rates in each content area. These data are essential to the collaborative team as they plan the instructional program.

Several sources provide detailed information concerning the development, implementation, and interpretation of CBM measures. (See Shinn & Hubbard, 1993, and Deno & Fuchs, 1988, for detailed descriptions for designing, administering, and analyzing CBM measures.)

Should We Modify the Curriculum?

To the collaborative team, the range of possible responses to this question seems overwhelming. As the instructional leader, the building administrator can guide the collaborative team in decisions regarding the modification of curriculum for students with mild disabilities.

The need to modify or adapt the curriculum for students with mild disabilities is well documented (Choate, 1993; Hammill & Bartel, 1995; Langone, 1990; Olson & Platt, 1992; Palloway, Patton, Epstein, & Smith, 1993). Unfortunately, the traditional approach has often been one of "additive accommodations" to lesson delivery. Specialized activities are added to lesson delivery based on the student's disability (e.g., learning disability, behavior disability, mental disability) and/or the student's deficits (e.g., attention, memory, motivation). The problem with this approach to curriculum modification is that (a) accommodations are based on assumed student problems and weaknesses and (b) the adjustments reside in the delivery, not the development, stage of instruction.

A more effective approach to curriculum modification would focus on adaptations in the instructional *planning* stage. Furthermore, the approach would result in modifications based on maximizing the student's *strengths and abilities* within the instructional context. This process begins with the collaborative team asking several questions concerning the adequacy of the instructional plan for the student with mild disabilities. See Salend (1994) and Wood (1992) for detailed information concerning curriculum modification.

Lesson Objective

The lesson objective is a statement of intended learner outcomes. The lesson objective includes a clear description of the skills to be learned and the expected criteria for skill mastery. Although the classroom teacher may typically generate a single objective for all learners, the planned outcomes may be adjusted to more effectively meet the needs of the student with mild disabilities.

1. Should the *scope* of the lesson objective be modified?

Options: The objective might be modified to cover a fewer number of skills or concepts for the student with mild disabilities. The objective may specify a different domain (i.e., cognitive, affective, or psychomotor) or taxonomy (i.e., knowledge, comprehension, application, analysis, synthesis, or evaluation) appropriate to the student's needs.

2. Should the *criteria for skill* mastery be adjusted?

Options: The student with mild disabilities may need additional response time (e.g., extra time to complete assignments), a different number or type of response (e.g., fewer written responses and more oral or illustrated responses), or a different type of lesson skill evaluation (e.g., true-false).

Lesson Introduction

The lesson introduction includes an attention cue, a review of previous learning, and a statement of the lesson objective and its relevance to the learners (Wood, 1992). The lesson's introduction is an essential component of the overall lesson planning process.

1. Should different or additional *attention cues* be included?

Options: The student with mild disabilities may need very discrete, distinct cues to facilitate attending. The teacher may plan to use cues from various modalities (i.e., auditory, visual, kinesthetic) or plan to increase the level of student involvement (e.g., ask the student direct questions, get student to assist in lesson set-up) to focus and maintain student attention.

2. Should the *review of previous learning* be extended?

Options: The teacher may want to include additional opportunities for the student with mild disabilities to recall and rehearse prerequisite skills or previously learned skills or concepts. Such extensions can be accomplished via individualized assignments (e.g., student listens to a "rapid-fire" review on an audiocassette, looks over a lesson summary sheet provided by the teacher, reads comments from previous day's learning journal) or group activities (e.g., a "round robin" review, reciprocal teaching).

Skill/Concept Acquisition

This component of lesson planning involves the selection of methodology to teach the skills or concepts of the lesson. Suggestions and recommendations for adapting instructional methodology for students with mild disabilities are available from a variety of sources (see Choate, 1993; Hammill & Bartel, 1995). The following questions may assist in the selection of sources and suggestions.

1. Should the *acquisition materials* be modified?

Options: Because much educational content is presented to students via print materials (e.g., textbooks), teachers may need to modify reading materials for students with mild disabilities. Strategies such as prereading questions, structured overviews, page framing, highlighting, adjusted difficulty level, or use of audiotapes may be appropriate (Meese, 1992; Salend, 1994).

2. Should the *acquisition strategy* be modified?

Options: The acquisition strategy is the planned method of imparting knowledge, skills, or concepts to learners. Students with mild disabilities often require additional, distinct, or adapted strategies to acquire the skills or concepts of the lesson. One approach to this type of adaptation, recommended by Wood (1992), is correlated with four specific teaching modes: the expository mode, the inquiry mode, the demonstration mode, and the activity mode. A second approach to modifying teaching techniques is content specific (e.g., adapted strategies for teaching reading, written expression, spelling, handwriting, math, science, social studies) (see Salend, 1994).

3. Should additional *media and educational technology* be included?

Options: The acquisition of skills for students with mild disabilities can be enhanced through the use of media and technology. Teachers may use microcomputers for computer-assisted instruction to supplement or modify acquisition strategies. A variety of audiovisual media, including overhead projectors, videotapes, and audiotapes, is also available to augment skill acquisition.

Skill or Concept Practice

Following the acquisition of skills or concepts, learners need opportunities to practice and apply the knowledge. Students with mild disabilities often need extended practice opportunities to rehearse and generalize skills. The practice may involve a variety of response formats and instructional grouping options.

1. Should student *response formats* be varied?

Options: Skill rehearsal and practice typically involve written responses from the learners. Students with mild disabilities often have writing difficulties that interfere with performance. Teachers may want to allow students other response formats to practice the skills they have learned (e.g., oral, illustrated) and/or provide assistance (e.g., peer proofreader, computer spellchecks).

2. Should other *instructional grouping* options be explored?

Options: The teacher may want to consider interest grouping (i.e., students selected based on similar interests); cooperative grouping (i.e., students working together to achieve shared academic goals); peer tutoring (i.e., dyads established for classmates to teach, practice, and/or evaluate skills); or reciprocal teaching (i.e., students assuming the role of the teacher to instruct peers). See Epanchin, Townsend, and Stoddard (1994) for detailed information concerning these instructional grouping arrangements.

Skill Evaluation

The skill evaluation is designed to measure progress toward intended learner outcomes. Based on the skill evaluation results, the teacher assesses individual student progress and plans subsequent lessons. The collaborating team may want to consider a variety of evaluation options for the student with mild disabilities.

1. Should *alternate evaluation options* be included?

Options: In addition to more traditional formats of written tests and oral responses, the teacher may plan to assess learner outcomes via projects, oral reports, or demonstrations. Self-correction or peer-based evaluations might also be considered.

How Should We Approach Classroom Management?

Classroom management is a complex process that cannot be approached from a simplistic point of view (Walker & Shea, 1991). Classroom management is frequently conceptualized solely as a matter of student control rather than a dimension of curriculum, instruction, and the overall educational climate. Research findings converge on the conclusion that teachers who approach classroom management as a process of establishing and maintaining effective learning environments are more successful than teachers who approach classroom management as controlling or disciplining students with disruptive behavior (Levin & Nolan, 1991). Despite differing views regarding classroom management, there is widespread agreement that students should be (a) on task, (b) behaving responsibly, and (c) showing good human relations. Therefore, classroom management involves processes and procedures necessary to establish and maintain an environment in which instruction and learning occur; responsible behavior is enhanced; and where the interaction of teacher, students, and subject matter is successful (Bauer & Sapona, 1991).

This view of classroom management is essential to the inclusion of students with mild disabilities. Although specific strategies and interventions may be selected individually to address problem behavior, they must be components of an overall, classroom-wide management plan. This plan should be designed to establish and maintain effective learning environments. The preventive-supportive-corrective model of classroom management is an example of such a plan. The model is illustrated in Table 3.1.

Preventive Level

The preventive level includes three classroom dimensions: the physical, instructional, and social-behavioral environments. At the preventive level, the classroom management plan involves arranging the physical environments, modifying the instructional activities, and structuring the social-behavioral context in an effort to establish effective learning environments. See Smith and Rivera (1993) and Jones and Jones (1995) for detailed descriptions of preventive strategies.

Physical Dimension

The physical environment should be arranged to maximize learning and reduce problem behaviors. Central components of the physical environment are the room arrangement, the room conditions, class rules, and transitions.

Room Arrangement. The classroom should be neat and organized. The seating should be arranged to fit the activity (e.g., desks for large group instruction, tables for small group discussions) and the

TABLE 3.1. The Preventive-Supportive-Corrective Model for
Classroom Management

	Preventive Level	
Physical Dimension	*Instructional Dimension*	*Social-Behavioral Dimension*
Room arrangement	Curriculum and	Group contingencies:
Room conditions	instruction	Independent
Class rules	Maximized learning	Dependent
Transitions	time	Interdependent
	Goal setting with	
	progress monitoring	
	Supportive Level	
Nonverbal	*Verbal*	*Task Related*
Planned ignoring	Modeling	Interest boosting
Signal interference	Name dropping	Hurdle help
Proximity control	Humor	Restructuring
Touch control	"I" Messages	Diversion/interruption
	Positive phrasing	
	Rule reminders	
	Corrective Level	
Response-Cost		*Time-Out*

purpose (e.g., in rows for independent work, in semicircles of chairs
for group participation). The arrangement of desks, tables, and car-
rels should allow for ease of movement, yet not create a sense of
density. Traffic patterns for routine activities (e.g., entering and leav-
ing the room, handing in work, paths to learning centers) should
be clearly established and reviewed with the students. Creating
work and learning centers also promotes productive class activity.

Room Conditions. The classroom should have adequate lighting,
heating, and ventilation. The room should be attractive, colorful,
inviting, and motivating. It should be a comfortable setting for
both students and teachers.

Class Rules. Four to five rules should be established and stated in positive terms. The rules should be jointly formulated and be specific. The rules should pertain to conditions that enhance learning and appropriate interactions. The rules communicate expected student behavior and stress the importance of student responsibility for behavior. The rules should be frequently evaluated to ensure utility and effectiveness.

Transitions. Procedures should be established to assist students in switching from one activity to another quickly and without disruptions. The transition procedures may include verbal (i.e., teacher prompts), physical (i.e., moving from one location to another), or structural (i.e., student timelines) cues.

Instructional Dimension

The instructional environment should also be arranged to maximize learning and reduce problem behavior. The central features of this component of the management plan are curriculum and instruction, maximized learning time, and goal setting with progress monitoring.

Curriculum and Instruction. The design and delivery of instruction are directly linked to academic achievement and student behavior. The teacher will want to select instructional methodology and materials to enhance acquisition of skills and to increase student motivation to learn. The previous section on modification of the curriculum should assist teachers in the selection of these methods and materials.

Maximized Learning Time. Students actively engaged in learning will have higher achievement gains and fewer problem behaviors. The time allocated to instructional activities and the rate of student engagement should be maximized. Student engagement can be facilitated by (a) gaining and maintaining attention to task; (b) fast-paced, fluent activities; (c) active, frequent, and concurrent participation by all students; and (d) high levels of teacher-student interaction.

Goal Setting With Progress Monitoring. Goal setting is an extremely powerful tool that enhances student motivation, focuses students' attention, and increases levels of students' task engagement. Goals should be specific, challenging, and attainable. Timely and frequent feedback regarding established goals is important. Progress monitoring used with goal setting can increase student motivation and a sense of accomplishment. The monitoring should (a) focus on the students' positive accomplishments, (b) require students to identify factors contributing to their success, and (c) provide opportunities for students to make positive self-statements regarding progress.

Social-Behavioral Dimension

Arrangements within the social-behavioral dimension are also important aspects of the preventive level of the management plan. The goal of arrangements in this dimension is to encourage appropriate, desirable social behavior from students and to minimize undesirable, inappropriate social behavior. One approach to achieving this goal is the use of group contingencies. Three types of available classroom contingencies are independent, dependent, and interdependent.

Independent Group Contingencies. Independent group contingencies are those that apply uniformly to each student, regardless of the performance of the group. For example, if students turn in completed assignments, they are allowed to participate in a 5-minute period of free time for talking to friends at the end of the day. This is a group contingency in that it applies to the entire class; it is *independent* in that one student's behavior does not affect any other student's consequences. An example of an independent contingency is a token economy system in which students receive tokens for exhibiting targeted behaviors. The tokens are exchanged for backup reinforcers at the end of the day, the week, or any interval of time.

Dependent Group Contingencies. Dependent group contingencies are those under which rewards are available for all groups members only when requirements are met by one member or a small subset of the group. For example, if a target student exhibits self-control (e.g., quiet mouth, hands to self) at a certain criterion (e.g., 80% of observation intervals), he or she earns rewards for the entire class. An example of a dependent contingency is the "secret student." A target behavior is defined (e.g., on task, in seat, fluency, accuracy), and the teacher randomly draws one student's name and keeps it secret. At the end of the specified period, the teacher evaluates that student's behavior against a predetermined criterion and rewards the class if accomplished. The procedure motivates all students because they do not know whether or not their name was selected. The teacher has to keep track of only the selected student's behavior, but the whole group exhibits the target behavior to access the reinforcer (Jenson, Sloan, & Young, 1988).

Interdependent Group Contingencies. Interdependent group contingencies are those in which a specific requirement for the reward applies to all members of the group, but the reward depends on the combined or total performance of the group, as well as the behavior of individuals. The group's combined performance is the criterion for anyone's receiving reinforcement, and all share equally in the reward. For example, a teacher might allow the class to participate in a special activity after *each* member completes an assignment successfully. An example of an interdependent group contingency is the "dot-to-dot" system. The teacher prepares a motivating picture fashioned out of a dot matrix. To complete the picture, the group draws a line from dot to dot. The picture should be easy for younger children (10 dots) and more difficult for older students (100-200 dots). A much larger dot is placed every 3 (younger) to 15 (older) dots. This is the reward dot. The target behavior is defined, and each student meeting the specified criterion (80% on task, 100% accuracy) draws a line between two dots. When the large dot is reached, everyone receives a reward. The greater the number of students meeting the criterion, the faster the group moves to the reward dot.

Supportive Level

The supportive level of the classroom management plan consists of strategies designed to reestablish an effective learning climate following off-task or inappropriate behavior. These strategies have been called surface management techniques (Long & Newman, 1980) designed to nip a problem in the bud by redirecting the student to more productive and appropriate ways of behaving. See Emmer, Evertson, Clements, and Worsham (1994) for detailed descriptions of supportive strategies. These strategies can be divided into three types: nonverbal, verbal, and task related.

Nonverbal

Nonverbal supportive strategies are low-key, subtle teacher responses to off-task, inappropriate student behavior. These strategies are designed to quickly and quietly bring students back on task and reengage them in the learning activities.

Planned Ignoring. Planned ignoring is intentionally and completely ignoring a behavior. This technique is used with behaviors that minimally interfere with teaching and learning.

Signal Interference. Signal interference is any type of nonverbal behavior that communicates to the student that his or her behavior is inappropriate. The signals should direct the student to a more appropriate behavior (e.g., finger over lips to be quiet, point to chair to sit down).

Proximity Control. Proximity control is any movement toward or standing close to the disruptive student. Often just walking toward the student is sufficient to bring him or her back on task.

Touch Control. Touch control is a light physical contact with the student who is off task. When possible, the touch control should direct the student to the appropriate behavior (e.g., escorting a student to the desk, moving a student's hand back to the desktop).

Verbal

Verbal supportive strategies are also efficient, effective ways to reestablish the learning climate following off-task, inappropriate student behavior. The teacher has several options available.

Modeling. When the teacher notices a disruptive behavior, he or she finds another student who is behaving appropriately and recognizes that student publicly for the appropriate behavior.

Name Dropping. This strategy involves using the student's name within the content of instruction. As the student hears his or her name, attention to task is enhanced.

Using Humor. Humor directed at the task or instructional content can defuse tension in the classroom as well as redirect students to appropriate behavior.

"I" Messages. The "I" message strategy involves (a) a specific description of the inappropriate behavior, (b) a description of the behavior's effect on the classroom, and (c) the teacher's request for behavior change. The strategy is effective in increasing students' awareness of behavior and in redirecting attention to task.

Positive Phrasing. This strategy involves a request for appropriate behavior plus a reminder of the positive outcomes for that appropriate behavior (e.g., "If you do _____, our class can _____.").

Rule Reminders. When the teacher has established a clear set of classroom guidelines or rules, misbehavior can be redirected simply by reminding disruptive students about the rules.

Task Related

Task-related strategies reduce off-task, inappropriate student behavior by assisting the student with the task at hand. These strategies are particularly useful when students have become frustrated with assignments.

Interest Boosting. As the teacher observes a student losing interest or becoming bored with the task, efforts to boost the student's interest can be made (e.g., recognizing how much work is done or left, timing the student as he or she completes the task, discussing aspects of the task).

Hurdle Help. This strategy involves direct teacher assistance to the student who is experiencing difficulty. The teacher may work a few problems for the student, offer to write the answers as the student says them, or provide additional assistance to the student (e.g., a dictionary, a calculator).

Restructuring. Handing the student a different writing utensil, having the student circle the next couple of problems to complete, or changing the location of the task area are examples of restructuring. The teacher attempts to change some aspect of the task in an attempt to reduce frustration and increase the student's motivation to continue.

Diversion-Interruption. This strategy involves a temporary "break" from the assigned task (e.g., a quick trip to the drinking fountain; a few moments to rest or relax; a short, off-topic discussion). Once the student is "rested," he or she is directed to return to the task.

Corrective Level

The corrective level of the classroom management plan consists of strategies designed to immediately stop behaviors that significantly interfere with teaching and learning. Two such strategies are response-cost and time-out.

Response-Cost

Response-cost procedures involve the loss of a reinforcer following a disruptive behavior. The reinforcer may be an activity (e.g., recess, free time) or a token used in the classroom token economy program. Some considerations concerning the use of response-cost procedures include

1. The teacher must be able to withdraw the reinforcer once given (i.e., response-cost cannot be used with edible or social-verbal reinforcement).
2. The penalty must fit the crime (i.e., the number or amount of reinforcement withdrawn must match the seriousness of the disruptive behavior).

3. The teacher must be able to balance awarding and removing the reinforcement or tokens (i.e., not moving so many tokens that the student is "in the hole").
4. The student must clearly understand the response-cost procedures. (Jenson et al., 1988)

An effective application of the response-cost procedure was developed by Schloss (1983). This adaptation, called the 10-R Technique, involves the student analyzing his or her behavior and practicing more adaptive, prosocial behavior. Additional guidelines concerning the use of fines or response-cost procedures are provided by D. D. Smith and Rivera (1993).

Time-Out

Time-out is a strategy in which the disruptive student is denied opportunity to gain reinforcement for a specific period of time. A variety of time-out options can be used when students engage in behaviors that significantly interfere with teaching or learning. T. C. Smith, Finn, and Dowdy (1993) list several variations, as follows:

Time-Out at Desk. Following a disruptive behavior, the student is asked to remain at the desk but is not involved in ongoing class activities for a period of time. The student is denied the opportunity to gain reinforcement from the curriculum, classroom activities, peers, or teacher for that period of time. The student may be asked to put his or her head on the desk or simply sit at the desk.

In-Class Time-Out Area. In this variation of time-out, the student remains in the classroom but is directed to a separate area for a period of time. During the time-out period, the student is not involved with ongoing class activities and is not given an opportunity to gain reinforcement.

Out-of-Class Time-Out. Immediately following the disruptive behavior, the student is removed from the classroom and taken to another room. This time-out option should be used when the behavior continues to be reinforced in the classroom or area when the behavior is extremely disruptive to the teacher or other students.

Time-Out Room. In this time-out option, the student is removed from the classroom to an area designated as the time-out room. The room should have adequate light, space, and ventilation. The student must be monitored continuously while in the time-out area. This variation of time-out should be reserved for behaviors extremely disruptive to the student, teacher, or peers.

Time-out procedures are effective in reducing disruptive, interfering behaviors. The school should have policies and guidelines governing the use of time-out procedures. These guidelines should include (a) a philosophy regarding the use of time-out procedures; (b) staff training requirements, including descriptions of roles and responsibilities; and (c) documentation and data collection procedures. Detailed information concerning time-out interventions is provided by Alberto and Troutman (1990).

How Should We Evaluate Our Efforts?

Schools implementing collaborative programs should evaluate the effectiveness of such arrangements in several ways. The main focus of evaluation should be on student outcomes, but additional feedback from teachers, administrators, and parents should be considered as well. The authors outline the following evaluation areas.

Individualized Education Program. For students with disabilities, objectives mastered should be reviewed during the annual IEP meeting. A data collection form should be kept for each student, reflecting the IEP objectives.

Report Cards. Data from report cards should be reviewed for each student in the program. Each of the academic, social, organizational skills, and other areas should be included for review. The kind and type of data available on report cards may differ between school systems.

Student Attitudes. Assessment of student attitudes should be included in the evaluation. Survey topics might include preference toward being in a regular, resource, or collaborative classroom; opinion of the school; desire to participate in class; and willingness to work with other students. Topics should be assessed for both the disabled and nondisabled students in the class.

Teacher Attitudes. Attitudes of the teachers involved should be recorded. Classroom observations and discussions should be maintained for review. The assessment of teacher attitudes might include opinions of perceived success or failure in providing the curriculum content, increased learning for all students involved, classroom management, team efforts, and grading procedures.

Administrator Attitudes. The school principal and other building administrators should be interviewed to assess the leadership perception of the collaborative program. Administrative staff members should give their opinion of the collaborative arrangement's strengths and weaknesses, as well as specific suggestions and comments.

Parent Survey. One of the most important data collection aspects is the perception of parents regarding the success of the collaborative efforts. Their feedback is necessary to indicate if their child's IEP needs are being met through the collaborative approach and whether they have observed changes in their child's behavior.

The overall atmosphere within a school determines the extent to which collaborative efforts will be accepted, employed, and successful. The *regular educators'* attitudes toward inclusion are essential determinants of the program's success. The *special educator's* provision of support and assistance is critical to effective collaboration. *Related service personnel* must be willing and available participants in program planning and delivery. The *parents* of children with disabilities must be willing to place their children in general classrooms and assured of appropriate support and individualization. *Students without disabilities* must be given information and experiences designed to (a) familiarize them with the characteristics and needs of children and youth with disabilities, (b) foster more accepting attitudes toward individuals with disabilities, and (c) promote better interactions between disabled and nondisabled children. *Students with disabilities* must be maximally supported in regular education classrooms. And most important, a positive attitude and administrative support of the building principal must exist if students with mild disabilities are to be successfully included in regular classrooms and if they are to receive optimal educational benefits (Simpson & Myles, 1993).

Individuals With Severe Disabilities: Inclusion Practices That Work

Inclusion of students with severe disabilities presents unique challenges and opportunities. Although these students are challenged by a number of learning difficulties, they possess many capabilities. Students with disabilities enhance and enrich the school environment in many ways. They can teach those of us without disabilities as much as we teach them. In this chapter, the learning and behavioral challenges presented by these students will be described. The roles of professionals who serve these students will be discussed. Emphasis will then be placed on assessment and instructional strategies for including students with severe disabilities in general education settings.

The example of the unit on westward expansion described in this chapter was implemented in the fifth-grade classroom of Ms. Joyce Stanley of Russell Boulevard School in Columbia, Missouri.

Characteristics of Students With Severe Disabilities

Students with severe disabilities typically have moderate to severe intellectual deficits as measured by standardized tests of intelligence. In addition, these students are often challenged by sensory, motor, behavioral, communication, and/or health impairments. These students have slow rates of learning when compared to students without disabilities. They often have difficulty in attending to relevant features of a task. They need repeated opportunities to practice new material because of memory problems. Skills learned in the classroom are not likely to generalize to other settings in which no instruction was provided.

In spite of these obstacles, students with severe disabilities can learn many new and complex skills if they are provided with appropriate instruction. Although progress will be at a slower rate, these students are capable of learning many functional skills needed in a variety of settings in school, at home, and in the community. They are also able to interact and become friends with their peers who do not have disabilities. They offer individuals without disabilities opportunities to learn about the value of diversity and tolerance for individual differences. These students provide the same joys to their teachers and peers as any other student.

Roles and Responsibilities

The coordinated services provided by professionals representing a wide variety of disciplines are required for successful inclusion of students with severe disabilities. Because of the multiple learning and behavioral disabilities faced by these students, the services of regular and special education teachers, speech clinicians, physical and occupational therapists, and paraprofessionals may all be necessary. It is imperative that careful planning and clarification of responsibilities take place before inclusion occurs. Professionals must be able to communicate with each other and work as a team in developing and implementing instruction in inclusive school settings. Because collaboration among professionals has been discussed in an earlier chapter, the key responsibilities of various professionals involved in the education of students with severe disabilities will be briefly reviewed below.

The building principal plays a critical leadership role in inclusion. Some of the most valuable contributions of the principal are support, advocacy, and a positive attitude toward students with disabilities in the regular classroom. It is important for the principal to make clear to all that he or she regards students with disabilities as full members of the school. Other professionals tend to model the principal's attitude. They look to the principal for support and the necessary resources to serve students with severe disabilities in the regular classroom.

The special education teacher will share responsibility for determining appropriate instructional strategies and modifying the curriculum to meet the needs of individual students. Special educators provide direct instruction and act as resources to the regular class teacher in inclusive schools.

The regular class teacher works closely with special educators and related services professionals in developing the instructional program. The regular education teacher regards the student with disabilities as a full member in his or her class. The regular class teacher can provide an invaluable service by teaching understanding and appreciation of human differences to class members without disabilities. An incident of teasing may be turned into a lesson on tolerance. The regular class teacher also must have different expectations and goals for individual students. Whereas a math lesson might involve multiplication for the majority of the students, the student with disabilities may be learning to purchase a soda using the appropriate coins in the vending machine.

Many students with disabilities require related services, such as speech, occupational, or physical therapy. These therapists must communicate clearly with teachers and parents. Many therapists practice the *integrated* therapy model. Within this model, therapy is provided in the classroom and other school settings frequented by all students rather than in a separate and isolated therapy room. Instruction is incorporated into the routine activities of classroom and home.

Paraprofessionals, or teacher associates, are important members of the inclusion team. Many of these individuals receive the major part of their training on the job because few states have formal certification standards for paraprofessionals. These individuals provide individual attention and assistance to the student with disabilities as required. Their activities typically include assistance with individual instruction, transportation of students who are not mobile from one setting to another, and help during the transition time from one activity to another. Many paraprofessionals are also skilled in handling episodes of inappropriate behaviors, such as temper tantrums.

Finally, students without disabilities play an important role in inclusion. They can assist the student with disabilities as a peer tutor or coach during academic activities. They provide opportunities to learn social and communication skills in class and on the playground. They may be special "buddies" to the student with disabilities and assist before school, during lunchtime, or at recess. Students with and without disabilities often become genuine friends as a result of the opportunity to attend school together.

Assessment

The first step in developing an instructional program for the student with severe disabilities in the regular classroom is to determine what skills to teach. Assessment of the student's strengths and weaknesses is used to design an appropriate, individualized instructional program. Because of the multiple learning difficulties faced by students with severe disabilities, standardized tests are of little use to classroom teachers in developing instruction. Informal, teacher-made tests, known as criterion-referenced assessments, are used instead.

Criterion-referenced tests are designed to measure an individual's performance on specific tasks. No comparisons are made between students. These informal assessments provide information about what specific responses a student can or cannot perform relative to a given task. This information is then used to decide what skills to teach. Steps in performing criterion-referenced assessment are outlined below.

The first step in designing a criterion-referenced assessment is to decide what skills to assess. For students with severe disabilities, the emphasis is on functional and age-appropriate skills. Functional, age-appropriate skills are skills performed frequently by age peers without disabilities in a variety of school and nonschool settings. Examples might include how to write one's name, use of the telephone, how to make purchases, how to cook and clean, appropriate social interactions, how to play a game, and, for older students, skills required on a job.

Four areas, known as functional domains (Brown et al., 1979), are analyzed for tasks emphasized in assessment and instruction. These four domains represent general areas of everyday life in which most people have to learn to function. They are the domestic, vocational, community and school access, and recreation-leisure domains. Examples of tasks representative of each of these domains, respectively, might include making a bed, clearing tables in a restaurant, purchasing lunch in a fast food restaurant or at school, and playing video games at an arcade with friends.

After it has been determined that a particular task is important for a student to learn, the task is subdivided into component steps. This process is referred to as task analysis. Each step, an observable and measurable response, is written down in the sequence in which it occurs in order to perform the entire task. Beside each written response is the number in which it occurs in the sequence.

The teacher then asks the student to perform each step in the task analysis (e.g., "Seth, pick up the quarter"). The teacher can then document which steps the student can or cannot perform by marking the number of each correctly performed response. An example of a task analysis for purchasing a can of fruit juice from a vending machine, along with a corresponding data sheet, is displayed in Figure 4.1. Browder (1987) provided an excellent description of strategies for the assessment of a broad array of functional and age-appropriate skills for persons with severe disabilities.

5. Check for any change in coin slot.	5555555555
4. Pick up can of soda.	4444444444
3. Push button to indicate choice of soda.	3333333333
2. Drop coins into vending machine coin slot.	2222222222
1. Match real coins to picture card for amount needed to purchase soda.	1111111111

Directions: Slash the number of each step performed correctly in the task during each trial. One trial consists of the opportunity to perform each step in the task without assistance. Circle the number of total steps performed correctly in each trial and connect the circles to chart progress.

Figure 4.1. Task Analysis and Data Collection Sheet for Purchasing a Soda From a Vending Machine.

Curriculum Modification

Related to the question of which skills to teach to a particular student with disabilities is the practice of curriculum modification. Students with disabilities in inclusive settings may work on some of the same objectives as students without disabilities. At other times, however, the specific objectives that they are expected to achieve will vary. Therefore, it becomes necessary to modify the traditional curriculum content.

One approach to curriculum modification that many teachers have found useful is the unit, or thematic, approach to instruction of learners with a wide array of abilities. Within the unit approach, all students are provided instruction on a broad topical area. Behavioral objectives developed within the broad topic are individualized to meet student needs. Using the unit approach to modify a curriculum is not unique to the field of special education. Rather, it is often used by teachers faced with the need to individualize instruction for the increasing degree of multicultural and cognitive diversity found in the regular classroom today.

An example of the unit approach to curriculum modification (and individualized instruction) follows. A fifth-grade teacher developed a unit on westward expansion. Her class consisted of 28 students, two of whom had severe disabilities, including mental retardation and behavior disorders. Students were grouped into "wagon train families" of three to six students each. Each "family" was given names, ages, and other identifying information about each member. Family members earned miles toward the final destination in California by correctly performing a variety of tasks across the curriculum. Each member of the family was expected to perform tasks that varied in difficulty.

Joshua, a highly competent student and the "father" of his family, was expected to earn miles by completing math problems requiring the use of decimal points. Latonya was required to write a book report on westward expansion using the computer. Miguel was asked to construct a covered wagon, using materials of his choice, and to calculate which supplies his family would need to carry for the journey. Jenna's assignments during this unit consisted of learning to cook and serve some of the simple foods, such as beans, that people ate on wagon trains.

Stainback and Stainback (in press) presented a wide array of curriculum modification strategies. They identified strategies currently in use in successful inclusion programs throughout the United States. Ryndak and Alper (in press) described a systematic process of curriculum content modification for inclusive school settings. They provided a detailed description of curriculum modification strategies that may be used with topics traditionally included in regular and special education curricula.

Instructional Strategies

After determining which skills to teach, instructional strategies are considered and selected. A variety of instructional strategies have been developed in recent years and documented as effective in teaching students with severe disabilities. These teaching strategies are based on observable and measurable behaviors and are referred to as "best practices" because of their effectiveness. Although a thorough discussion of best practices is beyond the scope of this chapter, the interested reader is referred to Cipani and Spooner (1995); Schloss, Smith, and Schloss (1995); and Snell (1993) for excellent discussions and examples.

Task analysis, referred to above, is usually the first step in designing an instructional program for students with severe disabilities. A task is subdivided into each of the steps that must be performed to complete the entire task. Each step is written as an observable and measurable behavior in the sequence in which it is performed. Each task analysis is developed based on the abilities of the individual student. For example, a task analysis for preparing a simple meal might consist of many steps for the student who has little knowledge or experience with this task. The same task would need to be divided into only a few steps for the student who had more abilities and prior experience with cooking.

After the task analysis is written, the teacher begins instruction by providing the student with discrete cues. A cue is any stimulus that provides the student with information about correct performance. Discrete cues are very clear and concise. For example, rather than saying, "Pat, shape up and go to work," the teacher will say, "Pat, pick up the screwdriver by the handle."

Using clear and concise cues is particularly important with students with severe disabilities. These students often have communication and language impairments. They may have difficulty following lengthy verbal instructions. Similarly, they will have difficulty in following cues that are used inconsistently by different teachers.

A discrete cue can be any stimulus that provides specific information about expected performance to a student. The cue may be verbal (e.g., "Push the button that says Coke"), visual (e.g., showing the student a picture of what to do or modeling the correct action), or physical (e.g., pointing or gesturing).

Sometimes a student fails to make the correct response after a discrete cue is provided. The teacher states, "Lech, open the box of macaroni and cheese," and Lech does not respond. The teacher will then need to use the system of least prompts (Schloss, Smith, & Schloss, 1995). The system of least prompts involves providing the minimal amount of assistance necessary for the student to perform the correct step. An example follows.

If, after giving Lech a verbal instruction, no response occurs within a reasonable amount of time (e.g., 5 seconds), the teacher may model or imitate the expected behavior to Lech. The teacher demonstrates the behavior he or she wants the student to perform and repeats the verbal cue. If the student makes no response after the modeling prompt within the specified time interval, the teacher may point or gesture to the box of macaroni and repeat the verbal cue. If there is still no response, the teacher may then need to place his or her hands on the hands of the student and manually guide him or her through the task.

In using the system of least prompts, two points should be kept in mind. First, it is important to specify the exact time interval during which the student is provided the opportunity to respond. This interval may vary from student to student but should always be consistent for the same student. The time interval should be long enough to offer the student the chance to perform the response. If the time interval is too long, however, the student may stop paying attention or engage in inappropriate behavior.

Second, the teacher should always begin with the least amount of assistance possible (i.e., allowing the student to self-initiate the correct response). More assistance is then provided following the sequence illustrated above. This assures that the student has the opportunity to perform with as much independence as possible.

During the instructional process, reinforcement for correct performance will need to be provided. Reinforcement is usually defined as following the desired or appropriate behavior of a student with some consequence that is perceived as pleasurable by the student. A student who completes work on time may be allowed a few minutes of free time.

In using reinforcement as a means of providing the student with feedback about his or her performance, the teacher will have to make two decisions. First, the particular reinforcer to be used needs to be determined on an individual basis. Anything that an individual student finds pleasurable may be used as a reinforcer. Stickers, verbal praise, edible items, social praise, free time, special certificates of recognition, and serving as the teacher's helper have all been used with certain students. However, the teacher should not assume that any one reinforcer will be perceived as pleasurable by all students.

It is a good idea to use natural, rather than artificial, reinforcers as much as possible. A natural reinforcer is some naturally occurring and pleasant aspect of a task, such as eating the brownies after preparing them or enjoying the appearance of an organized and tidy room after cleaning. An artificial reinforcer may be pleasurable for a student but is not typically associated with a specific task. Points and tokens represent artificial reinforcers. Artificial reinforcers may be effective initially, particularly when used in teaching tasks for which there are no naturally occurring reinforcers. They should be delivered less and less frequently as the student learns to master the task.

The second decision regarding reinforcement is how frequently an individual student should be reinforced. A good rule of thumb is to provide reinforcement frequently when the student is initially learning a new task. Reinforcement may be provided after every correct response, after every few correct responses, or after every short time interval during which the student remains appropriately engaged in the activity. The reinforcer may then be gradually faded, or provided less frequently, when the goal is to maintain behavior that the student has learned how to perform.

Options for Grouping Students

There are several options for grouping students that the teacher will want to consider in the regular classroom in which one or two students with severe disabilities are members. Traditionally, students in the American educational system have been grouped by ability level, a practice referred to as homogeneous grouping. This practice has been questioned by some educators, however, even in classes of students without disabilities. Students can learn from each others' differences as well as similarities.

There are several advantages to grouping students on the basis of age, a shared interest, or common assignment instead of on the basis of equal ability level. First, a student may have to learn material in more depth to teach it to a student of lower ability. Second, grouping students of varying abilities together for instructional purposes may increase their sensitivity and tolerance for human differences. Understanding and tolerance for difference are increasingly important in a pluralistic society. Third, heterogeneous grouping in which some students have instructional responsibility may free up some of the teacher's time.

There are several options for heterogeneous grouping in the inclusive classroom that the teacher may want to consider. First, some activities lend themselves to large groups of students with minimal supervision. Examples might include listening to a story, watching a movie or videotape, or listening to a guest speaker. These are activities that, if selected carefully, can be shared and enjoyed by students with and without disabilities without demanding a great deal of teacher time or attention.

Cooperative learning (Johnson & Johnson, 1983) is another option for grouping small numbers of students who vary in ability level. Cooperative learning groups work together on a common assignment or a project based on an interest shared by the group. Students have a group goal. The group, rather than individual members of the group, is rewarded for satisfactory performance. Each member of the group has a specific task or assignment that assists the group in meeting its overall goal. Cooperative learning groups are not permanent but may be formed and re-formed depending on the instructional purpose. A student may be a member of more than one cooperative learning group at a time. The wagon train families created as a part of the unit on westward expansion mentioned above were cooperative learning groups.

Peer tutoring may also be used as an alternative grouping strategy in the inclusive classroom. Students are paired, and one student plays the role of tutor, or coach, for another student. Peer tutors as young as 3 and 4 years old have been taught to teach skills, provide prompts and reinforcers, and collect data.

Peer tutoring may be used to teach a wide variety of skills across the curriculum. Peer tutors may be at the same ability level or above or below the ability level of the student they are coaching. Students in these pairs may also alternate the role of tutor.

Special buddy systems (Strully & Strully, 1985) have also been used successfully to group students with and without disabilities. In this arrangement, a student without disabilities is assigned as a buddy to assist a student with disabilities in a specific activity.

Special buddies may be assigned to recess or lunch hour, before or after school, on the school bus, or during a portion of class time. The role of the special buddy is to play the role of a helpful friend, rather than serve as a teacher.

Special buddy systems are used frequently in the areas of recreation-leisure skills, social skills, and during a wide variety of extracurricular activities. Many educators have observed an unexpected benefit of these arrangements. Although a special buddy system may be initially arranged or assigned by the teacher, the students involved form true friendships in many cases.

Scheduling and Transitions
in Inclusive School Settings

How to schedule daily activities and how to handle the transition time between activities in the inclusive school are questions that must be considered carefully. Many students with disabilities have short attention spans, and many have limited physical strength and stamina because of health problems. Students with and without disabilities often have difficulty in maintaining appropriate behavior during unstructured time and when they may be physically moving from one part of the room or building to another.

Scheduling of activities throughout the day can follow the same general guidelines for students with and without disabilities. First, the teacher will have to determine what constitutes a reasonable amount of time for a particular student to be expected to engage in appropriate behavior. Some students with disabilities can attend to a task for very short amounts of time initially (e.g., 10 minutes). These students need to have very short, structured periods that are gradually lengthened.

Second, the teacher can explain that some activities are negotiable and others are not. Certain tasks, such as academic lessons and classroom chores, simply have to be done. Other activities, such as how to use free time or what to do during a holiday party, can be decided upon with major input from the students. A balance of negotiable and nonnegotiable activities teaches responsibility and the ability to make prudent choices.

Third, it is usually wise to schedule activities that are not pre-ferred by the student earlier in the day. A student who detests math will probably do so even more at the end of the day, when he or she may feel tired and frustrated. The same student probably will not want to face math the first thing in the morning.

Fourth, preferred activities can be alternated in the daily sched-ule with nonpreferred activities. In this way, the teacher can use Premack's principle, or the idea that a desired activity can be used to reward completion of a nonpreferred activity (e.g., "Finish your social studies lesson, and then you may go to the library to check out a book").

Some teachers, especially those at the secondary level, have dis-covered that daily calendars, or planners, can be used successfully by students with and without disabilities (Schloss & Smith, 1993). Students can plan their day by writing down activities and assign-ments that must be completed, check off each as it is completed, and have their teachers provide feedback.

The daily planner has at least three advantages. First, it is a rela-tively simple device that provides the student with assistance in monitoring his or her own behavior. Second, the format of the planner may be altered to meet the individual needs of the student with disabilities. For example, activities may be color coded or rep-resented by pictures for the nonreader. Third, the daily planner is considered to be adultlike by many students because they have observed their parents and teachers using them.

How students use the transition times between activities will need to be carefully planned. Many teachers and parents find that periods of inactivity or in which the student is not sure what to do present the highest frequency of maladaptive behaviors.

The teacher should not assume that all students will automat-ically know what to do during these transition times. Although many students without disabilities learn which behaviors are ex-pected during unstructured time by observing and modeling their classmates, students with disabilities may not be able to do so.

It is important to clearly specify to the student exactly which behaviors are acceptable if an activity is finished before the period is up, and between activities. Students may be instructed to raise their hands or in some other nonverbal manner signify to the teacher when they have finished a task early. Appropriate behaviors between scheduled periods should also be specified. Whether or not students are allowed to talk between activities and specific areas where they are free to go will usually vary from school to school. The special buddies approach works particularly well in providing students with disabilities with assistance during the transition time between activities.

Technology

In recent years, a wide array of assistive technology has been developed to support students with severe disabilities in regular educational settings. Although it is beyond the scope of this chapter to provide a comprehensive discussion of this topic, it will be briefly addressed because technology is often a major support in the successful inclusion of students with severe disabilities. Assistive technology consists of any adaptive equipment or device that enables an individual with a disability to complete a task or gain access to natural settings. The adaptive equipment may be characterized as electronic or nonelectronic, computer assisted or manual, or high tech or low tech. Individuals without disabilities use a variety of assistive technology devices to make day-to-day life easier, including microwave ovens, exercise equipment, computer software, and convenience foods. Assistive technology may help individuals with disabilities in areas such as communication, positioning and mobility, functional skills at home and at school, activities of daily living, or vocational training. Some examples include wheelchairs, communication boards, calculators, and computer-assisted communication devices.

For optimal usefulness, it is necessary to carefully match a particular adaptive device to the characteristics and needs of the individual student. Selection criteria include, but are not limited to, the following factors:

- Individual capabilities of the student, including age, physical condition, and intellectual capabilities
- Cost

- Portability of the equipment
- Durability
- Flexibility of the equipment as the student grows and matures
- Repairability

With the technology revolution and the development of the microchip, for example, the range of adaptive devices available is rapidly expanding. Teachers, therapists, and families must work together to ensure that appropriate assistive technology is available for students who can benefit. This technology can greatly enhance a student's independence, interactions, and participation in inclusive school and community settings.

Evaluation of Program Progress

The purpose of program evaluation is to obtain objective information needed to make appropriate decisions about the educational program. Program evaluation provides information about which aspects of the program are working effectively and efficiently and which components may need modification. Program evaluation data also can be used to identify why a particular aspect of the program either works well or needs revision.

Program evaluation is an ongoing process. Although some evaluation data can be collected at the end of the semester or school year (summative data), other data will be collected at several points in time throughout the school year (formative data). Because the inclusion of students with severe disabilities into mainstream education is a relatively new and somewhat controversial practice in American education, program evaluation is critical.

Obviously, student progress data are an integral part of program evaluation. Several different types of student progress data may be collected, including the number of new skills learned and progress in meeting IEP objectives. If the skills taught to students are not functional or age appropriate, however, these measures may be meaningless. Most professionals in special education agree that the most relevant student progress data indicate the extent to which students with severe disabilities have learned to perform functional and age-appropriate skills and the degree to which these skills have generalized from school to nonschool settings frequented by persons without disabilities.

In recent years, a considerable amount of work has been focused on identifying indicators of quality in educational programs serving students with disabilities. These program indicators of quality are designed to ensure the most desirable outcome of education for students with disabilities: that these individuals will be able to live, work, and enjoy leisure activities with friends in the community when they leave school. Indicators of program quality in inclusive school settings according to Sailor, Gee, and Karasoff (1993) include (a) full membership in the regular class, (b) joint ownership by both special and regular education, (c) outcomes-based decision making, (d) student-based services, and (e) site team coordination of services. These five characteristics of inclusion are considered to be guidelines. How they will be implemented will vary across individual students, school buildings, and according to the desires of parents of students with disabilities.

Full membership in the regular classroom means that students with disabilities are assigned to a classroom or homeroom in the same manner as students without disabilities. Their membership in a regular classroom begins at the beginning of the school year. Then, the necessary supports and resources are brought into the classroom.

Full membership in the regular class has implications for the meaning of least restrictive environment. Under more traditional models of education, the concept of the least restrictive environment frequently was translated to mean that the student with disabilities was moved to a physical setting that already existed. Students with disabilities were placed in resource rooms or segregated special education classrooms and moved to regular education settings only on the basis of their ability level. Full membership in the regular classroom assumes that the least restrictive environment is the regular class. Rather than moving students, resources and supports (e.g., paraprofessionals, related services professionals, adapted curriculum materials, and technology) are moved into the regular class to create the least restrictive environment.

The second quality indicator of inclusive schools is that owner-ship of the education of students with disabilities is shared by the entire staff of a school. The principal, special educators, regular educators, related services personnel, and other school staff are equally responsible for providing a quality education to all stu-dents, regardless of ability level.

Outcomes-based decision making is conducted on an individu-alized basis for students with disabilities. Individualized outcomes, or performance standards, for a student with severe disabilities in a regular classroom may be similar to those of students without disabilities. For example, all students may be expected to meet the same academic or social skill objective in some cases, with the stu-dent with disabilities receiving additional support. All students are expected to learn to write their names in kindergarten. The student with disabilities may learn to write his or her name using a com-puter. In other instances, all students may be working in the same thematic area, such as a unit on managing money, but learning ob-jectives will be individualized. Most students will work on balanc-ing a checking account and budgeting, whereas the student with severe disabilities may be learning to make small purchases in the school cafeteria.

Student-based services are provided according to the unique learning needs of the student, rather than on the basis of what is available for the typical student. Student-based services such as physical and speech therapy are delivered in the regular classroom rather than in isolated therapy rooms. In this way, related services personnel can work hand in hand with special and regular class teachers and students. This model of providing services also facili-tates incorporating newly learned skills into normal daily activities.

Finally, site team coordination of services is a hallmark of suc-cessful inclusionary schools. The entire educational team for a par-ticular student attending a particular school building works together to implement full inclusion in that building. Site team co-ordination implies decentralization of school policy. The building principal and staff have more autonomy in developing educational programs and support services. Members of the team will include the principal, teachers, related services personnel, paraprofessionals, and parents. Site team membership will vary for individual students with disabilities attending the same school. The site team can decide which options and resources will work best to guarantee inclusion of a particular student in that building. The site team also considers ways of infusing information about human differences and inclusionary practices into the regular curriculum.

Summary

In this chapter, the inclusion of students with severe disabilities into regular classes has been discussed. Some of the unique challenges for educators associated with students with severe disabilities have been addressed, as well as the roles and responsibilities of individual educators. Strategies that have been documented as effective in serving students with severe disabilities in the regular classroom were emphasized. Program characteristics that are considered to be indicators of quality in inclusive schools were referenced relative to program evaluation criteria.

Much more work is needed if all students, without regard to ability level, are to be provided full access to their schools and communities. The accomplishment of this goal will require the best efforts of everyone who has a stake in the American education system. Full inclusion holds the potential for all children to be welcomed into their neighborhoods and schools because they are our children—and our future—rather than because they have earned the privilege.

*collaboration
not just
co-operation, co-ordination*

Annotated Bibliography
and References

Annotated Bibliography

Ayers, B., & Meyer, L. H. (1992). Helping teachers manage the inclusive classroom. *School Administrator, 49*(2), 30-37.

Special education must become part of a unified educational system to accommodate today's diverse student needs. New technologies and innovations, such as cooperative learning, whole language approaches, and interdisciplinary teaching, are discussed. Teaming approaches and ongoing inservice training for all teachers are a necessary component for inclusion to be successful.

Bergen, D. (1993). Teaching strategies: Facilitating friendship development in inclusion classrooms. *Childhood Education, 69*(4), 234-236.

This article discusses four strategies that teachers can use to encourage and to develop interpersonal skills of students when incorporating special needs children into regular classroom settings. Strategies involve (a) establishing a classroom climate that encourages peer interaction, (b) encouraging deeper friendships with diverse children, (c) providing social skills

*training, and (d) discussing the characteristics of good friend-
ships.*

Blackman, H. P. (1992). Surmounting the disability of isolation.
School Administrator, 49(2), 28-29.
*The La Grange Area Department of Special Education in Illi-
nois has had experience with moving toward inclusion for their
students with disabilities. "How-to" information is provided to
assist other school districts to be more successful in their efforts.*

Brown, L., Schwarz, P., Udvari-Solner, A., Kampschroer, E., Johnson,
R., Jorgensen, J., & Gruenewald, L. (1991). How much time
should students with severe intellectual disabilities spend in
regular education classrooms and elsewhere? *The Association
for Persons With Severe Handicaps, 16*(1), 39-47.
*Students with severe intellectual disabilities should be based in
the same schools and classrooms in which they would be based
if they were not disabled. However, this is not sufficient for an
acceptable education, and these students should spend part of
their time elsewhere. Nine factors to consider when determining the amount of time and the kinds of instruction that should
be provided in regular education classrooms and other settings
are addressed.*

Eichinger, J., & Woltman, S. (1993). Integration strategies for learners with severe multiple disabilities. *Teaching Exceptional Children, 26*(1), 18-21.
*This article reports the experiences of one school district as it
moved from serving students with severe disabilities in segregated programs to a full inclusion model. Year 1 focused on get-
ting started, planning, and beginning integration efforts, and
Year 2 on implementation of a structured peer integration program. Applicability of the full inclusion model is discussed.*

Evans, I. M., Salisbury, C. L., Palombaro, M. M., Berryman, J., &
Hollowood, T. M. (1992). Peer interactions and social acceptance of elementary-age children with severe disabilities in an
inclusive school. *The Association for Persons With Severe Handicaps, 17*(4), 205-212.
*Eight children with severe disabilities and eight nonhandi-
capped peers were observed in their regular elementary school*

classrooms. Acceptance of the students with severe disabilities seemed unrelated to social competence. Results did indicate that the children's social acceptance and opportunity for interaction are not uniquely associated with their status as individuals with severe disabilities, but with implicit standards and values of the students.

Ferguson, D. L., Meyer, G., Jeanchild, L., Juniper, L., & Zingo, J. (1992). Figuring out what to do with the grownups: How teachers make inclusion "work" for students with disabilities. *The Association for Persons With Severe Handicaps, 17*(4), 218-226.

Achieving full learning membership for students with severe disabilities requires teachers to provide all students with three crucial supports: teaching, prosthetic, and interpretive support. Furthermore, it is necessary to work within three inclusion parameters (curriculum inclusion, learning inclusion, and social inclusion) and through the development of teacher relationships. One student with severe disabilities was included in a high school drama class using proper supports within a cooperative teaching relationship.

Giangreco, M. F., Dennis, R., Cloninger, C., Edelman, S., & Schattman, R. (1993). "I've counted Jon": Transformational experiences of teachers educating students with disabilities. *Exceptional Children, 59*(4), 359-372.

This article discusses the experience perspectives of general education teachers who have had a student with severe disabilities in their classes. Teachers initially were apprehensive about having the student in their classes, but over the course of the year, their ownership of and involvement with the student's education increased. Helpful and nonhelpful supports were identified and discussed.

Haas, D. (1993). Inclusion is happening in the classroom. *Children Today, 22*(3), 34-35.

This article discusses how children were served before and after the Individuals with Disabilities Education Act. It states that goals should include social acceptance and providing children with the skills that they will need to function in everyday society. The article concludes with information on teaching methods that includes coteaching and team teaching.

Hamre-Nietupski, S., McDonald, J., & Nietupski, J. (1992). Integrating elementary students with multiple disabilities into supported regular classes. *Teaching Exceptional Children, 24*(3), 6-9.

This article describes four potential challenges to supported education as well as solutions that have been effective in meeting those challenges in an elementary school setting.

Hanline, M. (1993). Inclusion of preschoolers with profound disabilities: An analysis of children's interactions. *The Association for Persons With Severe Handicaps, 18*(1), 28-35.

This study involved the observation of three preschool children with profound disabilities in an integrated setting. Frequent opportunities for peer social interactions were seen, and these children engaged in interactions of comparable length to those of nondisabled peers. The importance of helping young, nondisabled children understand and respond to idiosyncratic behavior of peers with disabilities is stressed.

Hunt, P., Haring, K., Farron-Davis, F., Staub, D., Rogers, J., Beckstead, S., Karasoff, P., Goetz, L., & Sailor, W. (1993). Factors associated with the integrated educational placement of students with severe disabilities. *The Association for Persons With Severe Handicaps, 18*(1), 6-15.

Student, family, instructional, administrative, and logistical issues have emerged as five clusters of variables that appear to be associated with integrated educational placement of students with severe disabilities. This study identifies 19 variables within these clusters and empirically analyzes them and their potential interrelationship.

Kearney, C. A., & Durand, V. M. (1992). How prepared are our teachers for mainstreamed classroom settings? A survey of postsecondary schools of education in New York State. *Exceptional Children, 59*(1), 6-11.

Studies conducted over the past 5 years indicate that regular classroom educators are not adequately prepared to teach children with disabilities in regular classroom settings. Certification requirements of state agencies are insufficient and unresponsive to parent, teacher, and administrator recommendations. This study investigates the hypothesis that postsecondary schools of education may compensate by requiring more stringent coursework and experience.

Knight, D., & Wadsworth, D. (1993). Physically challenged students: Inclusion classroom. *Childhood Education, 69*(4), 211-215.

Provides suggestions for preschool, elementary, and middle grade teachers on mainstreaming students with physical and medical difficulties. Suggestions are given that focus on parent involvement, peer interaction, environment and training considerations, and instructional adaptations. The article also discusses topics, such as emergency care plans, that relate to making the inclusion in regular classes a nonthreatening experience for physically challenged students.

Kozleski, E. B., & Jackson, L. (1993). Taylor's story: Full inclusion in her neighborhood elementary school. *Exceptionality: A Research Journal, 4*(3), 153-175.

This article is an analysis of the experience of a student with severe mental retardation who experienced full inclusion in her neighborhood elementary school. It revealed that the student's opportunities for social participation and friendship improved, several adaptive skills were developed, the classroom teacher played a critical role in orchestrating the level of academic inclusion, and transition planning was essential.

McIntosh, R., Vaughn, S., Schumn, J. S., Haeger, D., & Lee, O. (1993). Observations of students with learning disabilities in general education classrooms. *Exceptional Children, 60*(3), 249-261.

Many educators agree that schools need to effectively integrate students with learning disabilities into the general education classroom. Students with learning disabilities are often characterized as "inactive learners," remaining on the periphery of academic and social involvement in elementary and secondary classrooms. Before providing specific recommendations about how best to integrate students into the regular classroom, this study seeks to obtain more specific information about the extent to which adaptation of accommodation for students with disabilities occurs across the grade levels.

Sailor, W. (1991). Special education in the restructured school. *Remedial and Special Education, 12*(6), 8-22.

Within special education, dominant reform trends have focused in part on achieving greater social and academic integration of students with a wide range of significant disabilities in general education schools and classrooms. Reform trends in general education have shifted to reorganization of school and district-level governance systems and to the manner in which fiscal and personnel resources are allocated and used at the school site. This article examines the basis for a shared educational agenda in light of current trends in reform.

Salisbury, C. L., Palombaro, M. M., & Hollowood, T. M. (1993). On the nature and change of an inclusive elementary school. *The Association for Persons With Severe Handicaps, 18*(2), 75-84.

Qualitative research methods were used to conduct an in-depth study of an inclusive elementary school with the intent of characterizing its context and practices. Such detail would provide valuable insight for those involved in systems change efforts. This school developed an inclusive community where policies, conditions, and supports were good for all its students. System change occurred slowly, intentionally, and within a collaborative process of decision making. The commitment and actions of the faculty in this school played an important role in developing important social values among the students in their classrooms.

Schattman, R., & Benay, J. (1992). Inclusive practices transform special education in the 1990s. *School Administrator, 49*(2), 8-12.

This article reviews the history of special education reform, discusses current ideas related to best practices, and illustrates a number of organizational characteristics typical of schools now using exemplary special education models.

Sindelar, P. T., Watanabe, A. K., McCray, A. D., & Hornsbuy, P. J. (1992). Special education's role in literacy and educational reform. *Teaching Exceptional Children, 24*(3), 38-40.

This article discusses the America 2000 plan and how regular and special educators can work together in achieving its goals. Procedures discussed are designed to help students with disabilities achieve greater success in mainstreamed classrooms.

Stainback, S., & Stainback, W. (1992a). *Curriculum considerations in inclusive classrooms: Facilitating learning for all students.* Baltimore: Paul H. Brookes.

This text focuses on how to promote inclusive education by designing, adapting, and delivering curriculum in general education classes. The goal of inclusive schools is to ensure that all students, including those who have been labeled severely dis-

abled, chronically disruptive, typical, gifted, or at risk, are accepted and included as equal members of the school community.

Stainback, S., & Stainback, W. (1992b). Including students with severe disabilities in the regular classroom curriculum. *Preventing School Failure, 37*(1), 26-30.

This article suggests strategies that general educators, in collaboration with integration facilitators and other specialists, can use to include students with severe disabilities in the regular classroom curriculum within inclusive schools. Implementation considerations focus on a team approach, peer involvement, emphasis on functional skills, and educationally challenging all students.

Stainback, S., & Stainback, W. (in press). *Handbook of practical strategies for inclusive schooling.* Baltimore: Paul H. Brookes.

This book is a day-to-day handbook of strategies to be used by classroom teachers. It provides information on how to adapt grading and curricula to individual differences. A second section deals with strategies for dealing with severe behavioral problems. Building friendships in the inclusive classroom between diverse students is also discussed. The final section tells how special and regular educators can work together to implement all of these strategies.

References

Alberto, P. A., & Troutman, A. C. (1990). *Applied behavior analysis for teachers* (3rd ed.). Columbus, OH: Merrill.

Bauer, A. M., & Sapona, R. H. (1991). *Managing classrooms to facilitate learning.* Englewood Cliffs, NJ: Prentice Hall.

Bauwens, J., & Hourcade, J. J. (1995). *Cooperative teaching: Rebuilding the schoolhouse for all students.* Austin, TX: Pro-Ed.

Bauwens, J., Hourcade, J. J., & Friend, M. (1989). Cooperative teaching: A model for general and special education integration. *Remedial and Special Education, 10,* 17-22.

Browder, D. M. (1987). *Assessment of individuals with severe handicaps.* Baltimore: Paul H. Brookes.

Brown, L., Branston, M. B., Hamre-Nietupski, S., Pumpian, I., Certo, N., & Grunewald, L. (1979). A strategy for developing chronological age appropriate and functional curricular content for severely handicapped adolescents and young adults. *Journal of Special Education, 13*(1), 81-90.

Choate, J. S. (1993). *Successful mainstreaming: Proven ways to detect and correct special needs.* Boston: Allyn & Bacon.

Cipani, E. C., & Spooner, F. (1995). *Curricular and instructional approaches for persons with severe disabilities.* Boston: Allyn & Bacon.

Deno, S. L., & Fuchs, L. S. (1988). Developing curriculum-based measurement systems for data-based special education problem solving. In E. L. Meyen, G. A. Vergason, & R. J. Whelan (Eds.), *Effective instructional strategies for exceptional children* (pp. 481-505). Denver: Love Publishing.

Education for All Handicapped Children Act, P. L. 94-142, 20 U. S. C. at 1401 et seq. (1975), and the federal implementing regulations at 34 C. F. R. at 300.

Education of the Handicapped Act, P. L. 99-457 (1986).

Emmer, E. T., Evertson, C. M., Clements, B. S., & Worsham, M. E. (1994). *Classroom management for secondary teachers* (3rd ed.). Boston: Allyn & Bacon.

Epanchin, B. C., Townsend, B., & Stoddard, K. (1994). *Constructive classroom management: Strategies for creating positive learning environments.* Pacific Grove, CA: Brooks/Cole.

Gable, R. A., Korinek, L., & Laycock, V. K. (1993). Collaboration in the schools: Ensuring success. In J. S. Choate (Ed.), *Successful mainstreaming: Proven ways to detect and correct special needs* (pp. 450-469). Boston: Allyn & Bacon.

Garland, C., McGonigel, M., Frank, A., & Buck, D. (1989). *The transdisciplinary model of service delivery.* Lightfoot, VA: Child Development Resources.

Gersten, R., Darch, C., Davis, G., & George, N. (1991). Apprenticeship and intensive training of consulting teachers: A naturalistic study. *Exceptional Children, 57,* 226-236.

Giangreco, M. F., Cloninger, C. J., & Iverson, V. S. (1993). *Choosing options and accommodations for children: A guide to planning inclusive education.* Baltimore: Paul H. Brookes.

Hammill, D. D., & Bartel, N. R. (1995). *Teaching students with learning and behavior problems: Managing mild-to-moderate difficulties in resource and inclusive settings* (6th ed.). Austin, TX: Pro-Ed.

Howell, K. W., Fox, S. L., & Morehead, M. K. (1993). *Curriculum-based evaluation: Teaching and decision making.* Belmont, CA: Brooks/Cole.

Idol, L., & West, J. F. (1987). Consultation in special education: 2. Training and practice. *Journal of Learning Disabilities, 20*(8), 474-494.

Individuals With Disabilities Education Act, P. L. 101-476, 20 U.S.C. at 1400-1485 (1990).

Jenson, W. R., Sloane, H. N., & Young, K. R. (1988). *Applied behavior analysis in education: A structured teaching approach.* Englewood Cliffs, NJ: Prentice Hall.

Johnson, D. W., & Johnson, R. T. (1983). The socialization and achievement crisis: Are cooperative learning experiences the solution? In L. Bickman (Ed.), *Applied social psychology annual 4.* Beverly Hills, CA: Sage.

Jones, V. F., & Jones, L. S. (1995). *Comprehensive classroom management: Creating positive learning environments for all students.* Boston: Allyn & Bacon.

Langone, J. (1990). *Teaching students with mild and moderate learning problems.* Boston: Allyn & Bacon.

Levin, J., & Nolan, J. F. (1991). *Principles of classroom management: A hierarchical approach.* Englewood Cliffs, NJ: Prentice Hall.

Lewis, R. B., & Doorlag, D. H. (1987). *Teaching special students in the mainstream.* Columbus, OH: Merrill.

Long, N. J., & Newman, R. G. (1980). Managing surface behavior of children in school. In N. J. Long, W. C. Morse, & R. G. Newman (Eds.), *Conflict in the classroom: The education of emotionally disturbed children* (4th ed.). Belmont, CA: Wadsworth.

Maloney, M. (1994). *Full inclusion: Heaven or hell?* Philadelphia: LRP Publications.

Meese, R. L. (1992). Adapting textbooks for children with learning disabilities in mainstreamed classrooms. *Teaching Exceptional Children, 24,* 49-51.

Olson, J., & Platt, J. (1992). *Teaching children and adolescents with special needs.* New York: Macmillan.

Palloway, E. A., Patton, J. R., Epstein, M. H., & Smith, T. E. C. (1993). Comprehensive curriculum for students with mild disabilities. In E. L. Meyen, G. A. Vergason, & R. J. Whelan (Eds.), *Educating students with mild disabilities.* Denver: Love Publishing.

Rehabilitation Act, P. L. 93-112, 29 U. S. C. at 794 (1973).

Ryndak, D. L., & Alper, S. (in press). *Curriculum content for students with moderate and severe disabilities in inclusive settings.* Boston: Allyn & Bacon.

Sailor, W., Gee, K., & Karasoff, P. (1993). Full inclusion and school restructuring. In M. E. Snell (Ed.), *Instruction of students with severe disabilities* (pp. 1-30). New York: Macmillan.

Salend, S. J. (1994). *Effective mainstreaming: Creating inclusive classrooms* (2nd ed.). New York: Macmillan.

Schloss, P. J. (1983). The prosocial response formation technique. *The Elementary School Journal, 83,* 220-229.

Schloss, P. J., & Smith, M. A. (1993). *Applied behavioral analysis in the classroom.* Boston: Allyn & Bacon.

Schloss, P. J., Smith, M., & Schloss, C. N. (1995). *Instructional methods for adolescents with learning and behavioral problems.* Boston: Allyn & Bacon.

Shinn, M. R., & Hubbard, D. D. (1992). Curriculum-based measurement and problem-solving assessment: Basic procedures and outcomes. *Focus on Exceptional Children, 24,* 1-20.

Shinn, M. R., & Hubbard, D. D. (1993). Curriculum-based measurement and problem-solving assessment: Basic procedures and outcomes. In E. L. Meyen, G. A. Vergason, & R. J. Whelan (Eds.), *Educating students with mild disabilities* (pp. 221-253). Denver: Love Publishing.

Simpson, R. L., & Myles, B. S. (1993). General education collaboration: A model for successful mainstreaming. In E. L. Meyen, G. A. Vergason, & R. J. Whelan (Eds.), *Educating students with mild disabilities* (pp. 49-63). Denver: Love Publishing.

Smith, D. D., & Rivera, D. M. (1993). *Effective discipline* (2nd ed.). Austin, TX: Pro-Ed.

Smith, T. C., Finn, D. M., & Dowdy, C. A. (1993). *Teaching students with mild disabilities.* Orlando, FL: Harcourt Brace Jovanovich.

Snell, M. E. (1993). *Instruction of students with severe disabilities* (4th ed.). New York: Macmillan.

Stainback, S., & Stainback, W. (in press). *Handbook of practical strategies for inclusive schooling.* Baltimore: Paul H. Brookes.

Stainback, W., Stainback, S., & Forest, M. (1989). *Educating all students in the mainstream of regular education.* Baltimore: Paul H. Brookes.

Strully, J., & Strully, C. (1985). Friendship and our children. *The Association for Persons With Severe Handicaps, 10*(4), 224-227.

Thousand, J. S., Villa, R. A., Paolucci-Whitcomb, P., and Nevin, A. (1992). A rationale for collaborative consultation. In W. Stainback & S. Stainback (Eds.), *Controversial issues confronting special education: Divergent perspectives* (pp. 223-232). Boston: Allyn & Bacon.

Van Reusen, A. K., Deshler, D., & Schumaker, J. B. (1989). Effects of a student participation strategy in facilitating the involvement of adolescents with learning disabilities in the individualized educational program planning process. *Learning Disabilities, 1,* 23-34.

Walker, J. E., & Shea, T. M. (1991). *Behavior management: A practical approach for educators* (5th ed.). New York: Macmillan.

Wood, J. (1992). *Adapting instruction for mainstreamed and at-risk students.* New York: Macmillan.

CORWIN
PRESS

The Corwin Press logo—a raven striding across an open book—
represents the happy union of courage and learning. We are a
professional-level publisher of books and journals for K-12 educators, and we are committed to creating and providing resources
that embody these qualities. Corwin's motto is "Success for All
Learners."